Y0-DVB-408

BLACK STUDENT/WHITE COUNSELOR

Developing Effective Relationships

by

Alvin S. Bynum

Dean *Emeritus*
Indiana University-Purdue University at Indianapolis

Expanded Second Edition

Alexandria Books, Inc.
Indianapolis, Indiana

1991

Copyright (c) 1987, 1991 by Alexandria Books, Inc.
Second Printing, January 1989
Expanded Second Edition, 1991

All Rights Reserved.
No part of this book may be reproduced in any form without
written permission from the publisher.

Library of Congress Cataloging in Publication Data:

LC: 91-71709

Bynum, Alvin S., 1926-
  Black Student/White Counselor

  Bibliography p. 137
  Includes index p. 152
  1.Black American college students--counseling
  strategies. 2.Black history. 3.Social sciences
  of the black community. 4.Case studies. 5.Manag-
  ing racism. 6.1980s update. 7.Summary.

ISBN: 0-944816-01-0

Printed in the United States of America

Alexandria Books, Inc.
P.O. Box 2768
Indianapolis, IN 46206

ALONE AND UNKNOWN

You are not me;
   I am totally other,
      And utterly separate from you.

Yet we are alike,
   In so many ways;
      We rejoice, we hurt, and we mourn.

The distance between us
   A million miles is;
      A truly unbridgeable gulf.

Yet I in my lone-ness,
   And you there in yours,
      Are closer than books on a shelf.

So different am I
   From any one else--
      And sometimes I feel so unknown--

Till I see in another
   That very unknown-ness
      And find that I am not alone;

If I see that you see
   Our difference as likeness,
      Then I know that we're neither unknown--

And we can, if we choose,
   Take joy in our knowing
      That neither of us is alone.

                    --E. Paul Sechrist, Jr.

"Alone and Unknown" is printed with the gracious
permission of the author who wrote it in 1980.

ACKNOWLEDGEMENTS AND THANKS

I wish to acknowledge and thank the many persons who had enough confidence in this project to urge me to finish it. Thanks to my wife, Marie, who, over the past five years, has shown great patience and understanding of my need to work evenings and weekends on this book. I am grateful to her for the time, space, and encouragement. Special thanks to Norm Merkler, an associate and friend, who taught me how not to be afraid of the word processor; to Sandi Pfeiffer, Paul Sechrist, and Joe Taylor (my long-time friend and mentor), all of whom told me years ago that this book had to be written. My deep gratitude also goes to my daughter, Lynn Marie, who carefully read every word of the manuscript with blue pencil in hand -- exercising editorial thoroughness. Any mistakes found within these lines are all mine. A.S.B.

DEDICATION

To my daughters, Lynn and Lisa and to all their black brothers and sisters, in the hope that they will someday equally share in America's bountiful harvest with their white brothers and sisters.

CONTENTS

Foreword

FOREWORD

Counseling black students is an important task that many white counselors need and want to perform in the most personal and effective way. Some white counselors, however, are unsure of their ability to reach the core of black students because of a lack of knowledge about the personal and cultural factors that affect black students' transition and adjustment to higher education.

Al Bynum has given us an important historical and cultural overview of the black students' world. He reviews some of the important literature on black history and culture -- a literature with which few white counselors are completely familiar. He shows us how to use this knowledge to enhance relationships with black clients. He emphasizes that white counselors can make a difference in black students' lives by helping them develop positive self-images and by creating supportive environments.

Dean Bynum outlines many specific strategies and techniques which white counselors will find useful. He urges the use of an holistic approach which recognizes all aspects of students' lives including the influence of special family ties and the impact of black culture and tradition. Understanding individual students' goals, needs, and aspirations is paramount to establishing the type of relationship that is necessary to build mutual trust and respect. Recognizing that all white counselors harbor some degree of racial bias, Dean Bynum offers suggestions for changing attitudes and behavior. Becoming familiar with black history and culture and reading black-oriented publications in order to appreciate the goals of black students and their families are only a few.

Higher education is still considered by the black community to be a desirable path to sharing in the "good life." Through Dean Bynum's insights we have access to some of the knowledge and practical techniques that will help us become more effective change agents on behalf of our black clients. Any conscientious white counselor who sincerely wants to help black students realize their full potential and their dreams will find in the following pages important ideas and strategies for helping bring these dreams to fruition.

Virginia N. Gordon, Ph.D.
The Ohio State University

BLACK STUDENT/WHITE COUNSELOR

Introduction

When students are culturally or racially different from their counselors, guidance and counseling services can generally be termed weak or unsatisfactory. This condition results basically from a limited cultural awareness on the part of the counselor -- thus producing ineffective interpersonal relationships. Competencies such as human awareness and good communication skills in meeting with persons of a different race unfortunately are not taught in most formal counselor education programs. There appears to be an erroneous assumption that if the counselor is only sincere, then all will be well. Counselors need to and want to be of equal service to all their clients, but often the topic of race or ethnicity is either ignored or given little emphasis in textbooks and graduate training curricula for school counselors. Much more is needed.

Hopefully, this book will open the door to the topic of counseling across racial lines through its organization and presentation of researched data and through the relating of personal experiences gained over the years by the author and other practitioners. It should help counselors (and other people helpers) recognize and appreciate the cultural differences and social sciences of their clients and how to use this knowledge to bring positives to the relationship. It is important for counselors to focus on the value of cultural differences and to help the client to achieve his or her desired academic and/or life goals.

Rather than use the negative pathological approach to the difference in human attributes, this book will use a historical, sociocultural avenue. By the use of such knowledge, counselors will be able to upgrade their own human relations skills particularly by learning how to talk, listen, and relate to black clients--expressly by using meaningful operational terms rather than cold, theoretical phrases. The reader will find that this book is not a report on a statistical study but rather, a guiding document written especially for practicing professionals to use. So, if the reader can look beyond both the traditional academic expectations of manuscript writing and the use of professional jargon and simply read with the intention to act positively on my frequent first person suggestions for counseling improvement, then this book will have served well.

If dedicated white counselors really understand and appreciate the social sciences of their black clients, then better communication should take place and the client will perceive the counselor as a caring person who is genuinely interested in his or her development.

This book will focus on Black American students and their experiences on predominantly white college campuses. Student needs and perceptions will also be examined in the context of the surrounding white environment in an even larger, dominant white society.

As one might expect, my own perspective is that of a Black American educator-counselor-administrator who believes that cultural attributes may serve to enhance the relationship rather than become barriers between black students and white counselors. With a slow but continuing effort in the United States to move forward with desegregation of educational facilities and programs, this, I believe, is the right time to help all school personnel enter into positive relationships with black students as honest, sensitive, and knowledgeable persons. It is my hope that the suggestions found within this book will help counselors, teachers, and administrators gain an enhanced knowledge of the black community's social sciences and, thereby, better assist these deserving students toward their own academic success. A.S.B.

ONE

THE AFRICAN DAWN BREAKS

BACKGROUND

Some background information may be in order to set the stage for understanding the social sciences of persons of the black community. It is, thus, necessary to begin at the beginning -- African roots. It is not possible to include here a full, detailed explanation as to why and how blacks became a part of this country. Instead of attempting a course in Black American History, some supplemental readings are suggested in the **Selected Reading List**, which is annotated especially for this purpose. Among those on that list are two distinguished black historians: John Hope Franklin (1967), and Benjamin Quarles (1964). Both give clear and articulate accounts of the involuntary arrival of blacks, their subsequent slavery, and finally, their integral participation in helping America develop in both slave and free states.

AFRICAN CIVILIZATIONS

Before the first white explorer set foot in the New World, blacks flourished in their own civilizations throughout the vast "Dark Continent" of Africa. Ancient kingdoms and peoples had established many cultural, educational, social, legal, ethical, religious, and moral dogmas and models for subsequent generations to emulate. Quarles (1964) notes that ". . . out of all the Old World (human) stocks that entered America, none came from as wide a geographic area as the blacks." The West Coast of Africa was the principal hunting ground for the slavers who wanted to cut their cost of operation by raiding the villages and the bush nearer the Atlantic Ocean where the ships waited to carry the unfortunate blacks in chains on the arduous sea voyage. The more ambitious slave traders captured a small percentage of human cargo in East African communities which were thousands of miles away from the ports on the West Coast. Many black slaves, thus captured and marched across the continent, did not survive the trip through desert, rain forest, crocodile-infested streams, and over mountain ranges.

Since he was of no single tribe or nation, the ancestor of the American black presents no singular physical type. They were, in fact, like the hues of the rainbow -- dark-skinned like the tall, brooding Ashanti of the north or lighter-skinned like the shorter Bantu from the Congo. Such variety in nationality, language, customs, culture, dress, religion, and physical types defied myths such as a single African personality or even a common tongue. The devious slave trader practiced "divide and conquer" tactics by mixing these separate groups of humans to promote confusion and, thereby, maintain control. Families were broken up deliberately, and young voluptuous girls and women were set aside for the sexual sport of the sailors aboard ship. There are recorded instances of individual suicides by women thus violated and many cases of infanticide by the mothers who gave birth to babies aboard ship. Rather than face a life of slavery, these mothers, in desperation, would leap overboard with the infant into the angry sea, and both would drown.

SLAVE TRADE

The early slave trade became so profitable that it was known as "The Golden Triangle." This was primarily an economic venture principally participated in by Euro-whites who provided the first side of the triangle by sending ships, loaded with metal and other manufactured hard goods, to African ports to be sold or exchanged for black slaves. The slaves then would be packed on board the same ships -- refitted with chains and irons for the long passage to America. Once in the New World, the slaves were sold to dealers in the trade for public resale to farm and plantation owners. Most were purchased for use as free labor in the Southern agricultural areas of America. Once more the ships were refitted to take on cargoes of tobacco and raw cotton from the plantation ports for the mills of England and other industrialized European nations. All three sides of the triangle would be completed and the process started over again.

TWO

A LONG PERIOD OF CULTURAL DENIAL

SLAVES DENIED OWN CULTURE

From 1619, when the first purchased blacks were debarked at Jamestown, until the end of the Civil War in 1865, generations of slavery and culture denial permeated the South of the United States. Not only did the white masters on the farms and plantations forbid marriages and normal family development among the slaves, but tribal customs and religion were barred. It generally was assumed that the Africans had no religion because it was not Christian in foundation. They were, in fact, not heathen but either clung to the Islamic faith or to one of many African religions centered in nature. Black people had great respect and love for a particular Being who was greater than themselves. Some whites who owned slaves often misused the Holy Bible to justify white superiority and black inferiority. By doing this, the institution of human slavery gained religious support and, therefore, church approval, or at least a policy of noninterference.

SLAVES NOT DOCILE

In spite of the severe slave codes legislated in the Southern states and in the Caribbean Islands, there were numerous slave rebellions. Most of the uprisings failed to turn the tide but gave the lie to the myth that black slaves were a happy-go-lucky, docile group who enjoyed deprivation and lack of freedom. One famous uprising, known as "The Nat Turner Rebellion," was severe enough to strike fear into the hearts of the slaveowners. The exploits of the feared Nat Turner Band have inspired a number of pieces of literature, both historical and fictional. Some writers perceive him to be at least a folk hero, if not a martyr, for the cause of human freedom.

During all phases of slavery in the South, blacks were denied the opportunity to practice their African heritage and cultures. Their language became a tangled patois mixed with Pidgin English which amused the white masters who reasoned that blacks were not capable of learning anything but hard work under a cruel supervisor and the worst of physical circumstances. African religious rituals were expressly forbidden in order to fully control their lives, but soon missionary zeal emanated from whites who began extending some aspects of Christianity to the deprived blacks. The religious reaching out was limited first to the house slaves who were permitted to attend the services but sat in a designated section (usually the balcony) removed from the whites. White pastors were known to further the white control by misinterpreting the biblical passage from Apostle Paul's exhortation on civility to the community at Corinth by preaching: "Slaves, obey your masters . . ."

Quarles (1964) stated that slaves practiced "day by day resistance" in a number of ways, often nonviolent in nature. For example, when permitted to sing while working, the blacks made up their own songs which, when casually examined, seemed harmless but might have contained a message of hope or even a condemnation of the white masters. Quarles continues that these Spirituals conveyed messages other than religious hope. The following songs, "Go Down, Moses" and "Pharaoh's Army," are good examples of the dual meanings conveyed by the simple words:

Go down, Moses,
    Way down in Egypt's Land,
    Tell ole Pharaoh
    To let my people go.

        O Mary, don't you weep, don't you mourn,
        Pharaoh's army got drownded,
        O Mary, don't you weep.

It is quite likely that the slaves identified their masters with Pharaoh in the Biblical story of Israel's harsh treatment while under Egyptian bondage. They envisioned themselves as the oppressed people of Israel and prayed that God would perform a similar rescue. Quarles concludes that, whether the slave was singing about justice in this life or the next, ". . . He was giving expression to his discontent with things as they were."

MIGRATION WEST and NORTH

After the close of a great and bloody Civil War between the slave and nonslave states, black freedom was finally won. Thousands of former slaves, turned out by resentful masters, started migrating west and north to escape the devastated South, which could not support much life. The fields had been left fallow and were overgrown with weeds because of neglect during the war. Cities and towns were virtually destroyed by the fighting, and slaves, freed without funds, beasts of burden, or even food, left the white farms and plantations in long, walking caravans.

As groups of blacks headed out, some of them stopped in what seemed likely areas in free territory and established settlements and towns which prospered for some time (Quarles, 1964). The promise of a rosy future soon died in the newly established communities outside the South for a variety of reasons related to economics, continuing white racism and the rise of violent white supremacy groups such as the Ku Klux Klan. White dominated state legislatures treated the all-black towns with a form of benign neglect which effectively erected a tombstone over deep graves. Few of these communities exist today as viable, progressive towns.

BLACK CODES AND JIM CROW PRACTICES

After the Civil War ended and Federal troops were withdrawn from the Southern States, most white Southerners still believed that blacks were born inferior to themselves. According to Meltzer (1984), "By the Fall elections of 1865, prominent Confederates were put into office everywhere. Reconstruction was in their hands." The obvious plan to carry out a return to the status quo was the passage of ordinances called "Black Codes." Meltzer states: "These were adopted by state legislatures which in all but name restored the Black to his old position of slave." The codes permitted a form of control similar to the infamous slave codes which permeated the pre Civil War South. Quarles (1964) asserted in his discussion of post-Civil War history that "The Black Codes . . . were designed to take the place of the slave codes." There were statutes written which said: "Persons of color shall be known as servants and those with whom they contract shall be known as masters." Free persons of color were subject by law to indentured service if found without employment and unable to pay the arrest fine. Public vagrancy laws also abounded which gave law enforcement persons great power to arrest and jail any black seen moving about the area. White legislatures met and passed laws which constricted black persons in every manner possible, often under the guise of "Home Rule" and "States Rights."

A fire storm of protest grew over the Black Codes especially in the North, and led to many rallies and conferences by blacks and whites to obtain the vote and justice for all citizens. They wanted oppressive laws repealed and blacks given federal protection. Ultimately, there were some positive results. Among the gains made were the establishment of the Freedmen's Bureau in 1865 by Congress as an aid society for impoverished persons; the passage of a Civil Rights Bill in 1866 which granted full citizenship to the former slaves; and the all-important Fourteenth Amendment to the U.S. Constitution, also passed in 1866 and sent to the states for ratification. This addendum assured equal protection under the law for blacks. The Fifteenth Amendment guaranteed the vote regardless of race or color. It became for white Southerners a double blow as it attacked their notion of states' rights and the concept of black inferiority.

"Jim Crow" practices and laws were developed to segregate people by their skin color, especially in schools, public accommodations, housing, jobs, churches, transportation, and restaurants. The end result was that blacks were continually denied access to opportunities which were readily available to whites. There was no recourse since the socially based practices were supported by an oppressive set of laws.

The descriptive term, "Jim Crow", arose from the words and tune associated with a dance which black slaves sometimes performed. Its use in everyday language has declined since the Fifties:

> Once upon the heel tap,
> And then upon the toe,
> An' ev'ry time I turn around
> I jump Jim Crow.

While today's students are a long way from their slave ancestors, they have learned some lessons well. The slave was always playing a role, trying to survive in spite of the hardship which was heaped upon his head. He could fawn and feign servility. His face could become a mask which belied emotion, giving the impression of docility. He was, though, a seething mass internally, hating himself for having to demonstrate such apathetic and even stupid behavior before the white master. Counselors will often find it difficult to discern what is behind that mask on a client's face. It will not be docile or servile, rather it may be defiant, watching, and testing. It would be well for counselors to recognize and understand the lack of eagerness of black clients to engage in an intimate counseling relationship with a white person. The next step would be for the counselor to move forward with the development of a higher level of trust by being earnest and honest in supplying information and advice to the student.

THREE

GROWTH AND DEVELOPMENT

EMERGENCE OF THE BLACK COMMUNITY

Despite great odds, the new black American persisted
in group cultural growth through the adopting of much
of the wider culture's most desirable traits. There was
a rapid advance into graphic arts, music, poetry, and
prose which extended into the early 1900s. Some
historians refer to this era as the "Black Renaissance."
It is perhaps a misnomer in that the majority of black
Americans were not among that small, elite group of
highly creative persons mostly located in the Harlem
area of New York City.

The bulk of the blacks nationwide worked at ordinary
jobs and supported families by honest sweat like most
other Americans. They often were compelled to create
businesses which would serve the black community since
their needs were not being met by white businessmen.
Each black community eventually developed its own
churches, barber shops, funeral homes, service
businesses, and places of entertainment. Most were of
adequate quality but generally limited by the social and
economic system (reinforced by law) which forbade the
white lenders to finance or otherwise support these
businesses.

COURT ENDS SEGREGATED EDUCATION

America continued "business as usual" in terms of bad treatment of blacks in all phases of life. This was particularly true in education, social life, economic development, and political justice. In fact, the U.S. suffered through two world wars and an armed "police action" in Korea before the 1954 Brown vs. Topeka Board of Education decision by the U.S. Supreme Court struck down segregated education. The Black American's expectation of the Court's intent ". . . with all deliberate speed . . ." was high. It was perceived by many as an approach to an answer for many problems in this country. Unfortunately, this was not to be. By use of the legal appeal process and the passage of unconstitutional state laws in segregationist legislatures, the edict was stalled for years. The immediate period following the Brown decision was overspread by clashes between the segregationists and the integrationists. Much of the legal fighting on behalf of black plaintiffs was done by the National Association for the Advancement of Colored People and by other organizations that believed in the desegregation of America.

During the Sixties there were bombings of militant blacks' homes, churches and businesses. Innocent black children were maimed and killed by mysterious explosions, police dogs, water hoses, and even electric cattle prods in the hands of white policemen. This was a serious time in which a great personal price was paid by blacks in the South for a chance at freedom. Many of the gains made were the direct result of the real blood and tears shed by many young blacks (and some Northern whites) who dared to place their lives and futures on the line to march in protest, register to vote, and become involved in the political process in towns that had always been run by white segregationists.

Following the Sixties, which saw many demonstrations by peaceful, petitioning blacks and the infamous brutal police actions against them, there was slow progress made.

AFFIRMATIVE ACTION OFFERS HELP

The subsequent decade produced an era of federally imposed desegregation which spoke for the minority person in education, employment, and other areas of life. Significant inroads finally were realized as restaurants, hotels, and transportation modes began providing equal accommodations in response to the Civil Rights Act of 1964. It was clearly demonstrated that, in many locales, the idea of custom often outweighed the law in that no changes were tolerated until about 1966.

There was great hope in the black communities of America that the concept at the base of affirmative action would permit the active search for qualified blacks for entry into educational institutions of post-secondary education and previously restricted career fields. Beyond the simple termination of discriminatory practices, the concept of affirmative action is any measure used to correct past and present discriminatory practices so that discrimination will not recur and so that groups benefiting from such practices will cease to do so. Black boys and girls began to dream about some horizons never seen before in their families. This had a positive effect on upward mobility for blacks and continued through the early Eighties.

In 1978, the U.S. Supreme Court decision in <u>Bakke</u> <u>vs</u>. <u>University</u> <u>of</u> <u>Southern</u> <u>California</u> <u>at</u> <u>Davis</u> spoke to some errors made by the University which had set some racial quotas. This particular decision admitted a white student to the Davis (California) Medical School on the complaint that he was indeed a "victim of reverse discrimination." While it did not overturn affirmative action, the decision did, however, permit educational institutions to consider the ethnicity of the applicant in making admissions but not to establish quotas.

ACHIEVING SCHOOL RACIAL BALANCE

The latter part of the Seventies and the early Eighties were concerned with attempts to desegregate the public schools, both the lower grades and the universities. These were nationwide efforts since there were many school districts and institutions of higher education that had totally white enrollments or in some way had limited black access. The primary issue was that of busing of black school children, under court order, to distant schools to achieve racial balance since the Federal Courts repeatedly declared racially segregated schools as inherently inferior. State legislatures and even the U.S. Congress became active in an attempt to stop the busing but offered no other remedy for the basic, root cause of inequality. The prospect of universally acceptable solutions seems to grow out of reach the longer the issue is debated.

FOUR

A LOOK AT THE MODERN BLACK AMERICAN FAMILY

HUMAN AND BLACK

In sharp contrast to Moynihan and Glazer's limiting perception of Black Americans, Billingsley (1968) states ". . . We do not view the Negro family as a causal nexus in a 'tangle of pathology' which feeds on itself. It is indeed a subsystem of the wider society." Further, Billingsley asserts that it is extremely difficult for young members of the black family to learn how to become human and black at the same time in a white surrounding society. In order to survive, families must teach their young certain skills and behaviors which will allow them to remain black and moral. So the challenge is double for black parents and their children's significant others, for the child needs to learn to cope in a society which has not acted responsibly toward all its citizens according to the tenets of the U.S. Constitution. The sense of "peoplehood" as experienced by whites is shut off to blacks since they have a different historical identity.

Presenting a cultural approach to the black family's structure, Killens, in Three Perspectives on Ethnicity (1976), said ". . . there is a black psyche . . . and there is a white one. Our emotional chemistry is different from yours in many instances. Your joy is

very often our anger and your despair our fervent hope."
A clear explanation of the fundamental differences
between the two racial groups is the fact that most
blacks came to America in chains and most whites came to
escape their chains. Thus, continues Killens, "Your
freedom was our slavery and therein lies the bitter
difference in the way we look at life." Historians,
social planners, government officials, general citizens,
and professional educators who ignore or discount such
facts make the serious mistake of beginning from a false
assumption. It can only lead to an illogical, incorrect
conclusion, unless there is some corrective intervention
along the way.

FAMILY AS FOUNDATION

The black family system is the basic social unit of
the black community. (Please note that the author's use
of "the" in relation to the family unit is for the sake
of editorial convenience. It should not be construed as
a comprehensive description of all black families in
America.) Perhaps it is well to affirm at this point
that there is no singular form or structure to the black
family in America. In fact, it has as many different
forms as found in white families. There is great
diversity within the black family's makeup -- but that
diversity should not be taken as a negative factor.
Indeed, it adds to the vitality and individualism of
which this country is rightly proud. There is no
evidence of need for promotion of a "sameness" of
character or appearance. Life should be lived as
normally as possible with care not to infringe on the
rights of others within the society.
As the black family transferred from the slave
quarters to individual farms and small-town life, it is
helpful to note that subtle, as well as obvious, change
occurred within its structure. There was a rapid growth
of family units after the close of the Civil War when
freed slaves began their trek to other parts of the
nation where opportunities seemed to be greater. The
prohibition by white masters of slave monogamous

marriages was no longer in effect, and youthful black males could openly practice the romantic style of winning the hearts of eligible young women. Much of the courtship was based in the African cultural oral tradition in which the Griot, or village storyteller and local historian, also kept the community aware of the taboos regarding genetic lineage. Counselors who work with black clients should pay greater attention to their students' oral expressions in order to understand the psychological functioning of black people. As Thomas et al. (1972) report, "Much of black culture and psyche is an oral culture -- the blues, the gospel songs, the 'heavy rap', the sermon, and traditions have been carried on orally." Creative listening by professionals with a conscious intent to learn from others will be beneficial in the relationship building process. Counselors, however, must not ignore the basic principles of counseling which involve the recognition of the human condition and individualism in making wise decisions. Applying the fundamental methodologies found in the counseling theoretical framework plus specialized knowledge (such as that which follows) will serve well to prevent the development of an unconscious level of racial stereotyping and prejudice.

FAMILY PATTERNS

Billingsley (1968) listed three family types: 1) basic -- where there is husband and wife only; 2) nuclear -- consisting of husband, wife, and immediate children; and 3) attenuated nuclear -- where one parent is absent. Although this listing may seem very clean and box-like, it forms a point of departure. A more detailed subdivision by Billingsley consists of extended families, subfamilies, and augmented families. Social scientists explain the extended family as being composed of one or more relatives (and sometimes just friends) who function as a part of the basic family unit. The subfamily concept comprises relatives who join another family in the latter's residence (e.g., parents and

children of family A physically living with the parents
and children of family B at B's home). Augmented family
units generally form when boarders, roomers, or friends
who stay a long time join the household and usually
contribute to the financial upkeep. Billingsley also
maintains that black family structures seem to have some
homogeneity which grows out of the need for survival.
Therefore, many different types of family units may
emerge as conditions dictate. He concludes that the
simple nuclear family under one roof is, by far, the
form most observed in the black community in America.
It also happens to be the form which white America seems
to prefer.

There has been much publicity given to the notion
that the black family is rapidly becoming female-headed
rather than male-headed. Since this book is not written
to explore in depth all of the ramifications surrounding
controversial issues in the makeup of the black family,
the following list will simply introduce the reader to
their complexities: 1) teen-age pregnancies and
illegitimacy; 2) early marriage and early divorce; 3)
unemployment and public welfare; 4) the concept of
matriarchy in the family; and 5) impact of urbanization.
There are many variables contained in the powerful
forces listed which can and do affect family
development and may even contribute to its
disintegration.

Most black students' families will be found
statistically in the lower socioeconomic group which
comprises the largest segment of the black community.
The purchase of a house is a dream which is held dear to
their hearts. There is constant talk among black people
about "owning property" -- even if it is a few poor
acres somewhere in Southern farming country or a small
house in the city. The dream is to become a substantial
property owner and, through that medium, to become a
part of the middle class. The low sources of income for
such families continually deny them the upward movement
they desire. The economic condition of the country
which currently promotes high tech and few jobs
exacerbates the situation, driving the working poor down

into what Billingsley (1968) and other social scientists term a "permanent underclass."

Following the Puritan work ethic, the middle class black family is considered successful if, through team effort and two incomes, husbands and wives purchase a "good house," are more egalitarian in house chores, jointly discipline the children and hold a membership in a local church. Quite often both parents will have attended college and urge their children to go to college, too. Many times they become "affluent conformists" who mimic white-middle class families by giving music lessons to the children, having smaller families and belonging to an organization such as a mens' club or womens' club for a social outlet. Counselors should be aware that students from black middle-class families may come to the college experience with a liberal dose of what Clark (1965) called "the hidden curriculum." These students generally arrive with better rank in class from high school, higher SAT scores, and more involvement in the community and school activities. This extra font of knowledge and experience can put them ahead of their brothers and sisters whose low family incomes will not permit the purchase of books, magazines, newspapers, travel on summer vacations, and other advantages considered "normal" to the white middle-class child.

Having knowledge of black family differences based on earned income, white counselors should be able to assist black students better and more completely -- without undue expectations or complications arising out of the differences. It may be difficult for white counselors to recognize these subtle differences since most middle-class black students will not behave as "an economic superior" within his or her own student cohort. For them, survival comfort in a new experience such as college requires not displaying one's economic worth, thereby "fitting in" the group.

URBANIZATION IMPACT

Of all the change forces listed above, the one having perhaps the widest and greatest impact is that of urbanization. For at least four decades after the world entered the twentieth century, blacks migrated from the Southern farm and rural nonfarm areas into the cities where factory jobs beckoned and the dream of better education for the children seemed certain. Sadly, there were so many negative forces awaiting their arrival into segregated housing areas (later known during the 1960s as "ghettos") that multiple problems became the norm. New to the urban setting, black adults had to adjust to a new style of work, living, shopping, social outlets and the effects of crime. Of course there was serious family disintegration because of the effective elements of urbanization and as a consequence of intellectual, institutional, and legal racism. The city's ills produced, in great part, the split-up of the family when the black male could not find work to assure an adequate amount of financial support. This frequently meant that public welfare became necessary. Such financial help generally was not extended when the father of the family was present in the home. If he left the household, either by death, divorce or desertion, then the rest of the family might qualify for aid. The procedure was, and for the most part still is, supported or dictated by law. All of the negative forces facing black families in the cities create an atmosphere which fosters a group feeling of alienation in the midst of a metropolis.

RELIGION AS A SUPPORT

The black Africans had well-developed religions long before the white man visited the continent or started the slave trade. They were mostly of the Islamic faith or believed in a god found in nature, such as the sun, or an animal, or the mystical river or lake near their habitat. Thus, Christianity was a latter-day addition to the African's list of religious beliefs.

While in slavery, the blacks attempted to practice their own individual religions, but to no avail. The white masters would not permit their gathering unsupervised in groups out of fear of an uprising. It was not until many years later that the religion of Christianity was offered to the slaves -- but in a very limited manner. At first, certain male slaves were permitted to listen to the white ministers as they read the Bible and preached at the Sunday services in local churches. Having good memories, the untutored slaves would repeat what they had heard to their fellow slaves, using their own style of delivery. This gesture of Christian fellowship, while not fully embracing the slave condition, later developed into a "profession" for those who preached. Slave diaries and slaveholder records testify to such practices. In the few decades before the outbreak of the Civil War, there were plantations where a slave community was permitted to exist. Within these sub-social communities there were registered marriages, intact families, and the practice of genealogical integrity (Gutman, 1976).

With freedom, the blacks continued to seek the solace of Christian ethics in the continuing struggle for social and economic justice. By 1870 the Colored Methodist Church in America was organized as a branch of the Methodist Episcopal Church South. But since blacks were not welcomed into the white church parishes and congregations, it was inevitable that other organized Black Churches would come into being (Quarles, 1964). As an example, one denomination did arise out of a protest within the Methodist Episcopal Church which would not recognize the black yearning for inclusion in all facets of the faith and its mission. One of the early independent offshoots to develop was the African Methodist Episcopal Church, which survives today as a pillar of the black community all over the U.S. and the Caribbean Basin. Later other groups formed their own churches to satisfy the religious needs. Blacks are found basically within Protestant denominations with fundamentalistic theologies, while only a fraction of U.S. blacks will be found in the Roman Catholic Church.

As the black community grew within the larger white community, Christianity grew in America and by the year 1900 was divided along the color line even more than before. It is commonly stated even today that "the most segregated time in America is at eleven o'clock on Sunday morning." Despite this fact of current racism, the late Martin Luther King, Jr., wrote in a speech that

" . . . a religion true to its nature must also be concerned about man's social conditions. Religion deals with both earth and heaven, both time and eternity." (King, C., 1983). "Religious" black people seek denominations where the pastors preach the "social gospel" and integrate pragmatism with theology. Black churches are bastions of strength, hope, and courage in the pursuit of social, economic, and political equity. In general the black community continues to join and belong to an organized church which is usually located within a predominantly black neighborhood. Some metropolitan areas, though, may have exceptions due to urban renewal or the progress of the highway system which displaced both church and people through the acquisition of land needed for the construction project. Many times this political movement of black people and their institutions raised a charge of racism and persecution of the poor by the white power structure. As is often the case, black congregations thus affected are likely to purchase a recently vacated church structure formerly owned by a white congregation which is now moving to suburbia.

Hill (1972) asserted that: "Blacks have been adept at using religion as a mechanism for survival and advancement also, . . . the Negro church, (is) one of the most independent institutions in the black community." This was dramatically demonstrated in the earliest black settlements after freedom from slavery and into the turn of the Twentieth Century and that horrible period of black lynchings and racial hatred of the Twenties and Thirties. The black church often served the community as a haven from white harassment and abuse since it was generally dismissed by the white community as nothing more than a house of religious worship. On the contrary, it was indeed a meeting house for civil rights activities, a social meeting hall after religious services, and a source of charitable support for indigent blacks.

During the 1960s and early 1970s, the black church, particularly in the deep South, was the rallying point for peaceful marches against racial intolerance as well as the famous demonstrations known as "lunch counter sit-ins" in which young black people were courageous enough to dare to break the unfair segregation laws. Their ultimate victory is historic.

Many of the leaders of the black community came from the realm of the pulpit during decades past when the cloak of leadership was placed upon their shoulders. Some of these men and women later became famous and widely respected persons, in part because of their abilities to inspire, organize, lead, and develop other people for service to the general community need. Thus, the black church by necessity was fashioned into a fortress of support and protection from the real life negative situations created by racial intolerance. It remains very dear to the hearts of those in the black community as a resource in time of trouble and when counsel is needed for civic problem solving. It provides the religious and moral tenets necessary for living good lives, raising families and worshiping God. The church is also a place where good role models exist for black youth to emulate and a place where they can be developed into mature, productive citizens.

The white counselor who is aware of the closeness that a black youth feels toward his or her church will respect that relationship. Such knowledge can often lead to a community resource for the solving of certain student problems. As an example, most black churches have college scholarship programs or some form of financial aid for their youthful members. Frequently a student's needs may be met by the counselor contacting the church pastor, or lay leadership, and requesting assistance. Black church members still today strongly believe in the power of higher education for social and economic advancement of young people. Thus, the black church should be an important part of the counselor's resource list. (See: "Resource List.")

SOCIAL INTERACTION

Social change is always painful, especially for those who must give up or share life benefits because of the legal or moral rights of the aggrieved group. The social situation establishes the closeness of neighborhood and friends. When there is little or no social interaction between racial groups, then little progress can be expected. Billingsley (1968) notes that white middle class people know little about the lives, aspirations, and sensibilities of the black people with whom they daily work. This condition fosters fear of what their friends and other associates will think of them if they cross the color line in true friendship. The fear grows to the point of imagined ostracizing by family and friends. Yet many whites are quick to say: "I have no racial problems" while at the same time increasing the psychological and social distance between themselves and all blacks.

White counselors who succumb to an intellectual stereotyping of all blacks as poor and ignorant can lead themselves into a "serious error" which, according to Ginzberg (1967), may serve only to negate those public policies and practices which were designed to improve the socioeconomic conditions. While much of the black community is near or below the poverty line, there is a "working poor" and a middle class group that must be accounted for. Granted, although the majority of the black students who enter the nation's colleges and technical schools will come from economically disadvantaged families, they still have middle-class desires, goals, and hopes for the future. It is on this knowledge that caring counselors can build strong and helpful relationships with their black clients.

BLACK YOUTH AVAILABILITY

Since 1850 the U.S. Census has reported more black females than black males in the population. A drastic decrease occurred in the Seventies as a result of the enormously high death rate of young black men in the Vietnam War. This bodes poorly for the black female in terms of finding a likely future life-mate in the U.S. The outlook is, therefore, dismal, since black females are seldom chosen for meaningful relationships by white males. The overall social climate is still not fully accepting of mixed racial marriages or alliances. Black men find it perhaps easier to enter such a relationship

24

with white women, some of which last a lifetime, while
others break up early when the couple find it difficult
to survive in a social system that excludes them on
nearly every level.

In addition, the geographical distribution of males
and females throughout the U.S. is disproportionate to
supply and demand. There appears to be a different set
of forces at work in the geographic mobility of black
males and females as they move about. Census Reports
list only a few states where black men outnumber the
women. Those locations are in the West and Northwest
which are heavily farm-oriented and liberally sprinkled
with important military installations. Of greater
significance is that no southern or border states are
included in the aforementioned locations -- and that is
where the majority of black females live.

Many persons on college campuses witness romantic
attachments that blacks and whites have for each other,
and there are varied reactions to any public display of
affection between the races. Counselors should be aware
of the campus social system and try not to become a part
of a restrictive attitude which condemns mixed couples
simply because they are of different races. If things
are not going well in their social life, then one or
the other partner in the mixed couple may seek advice
from the academic counselor by dropping a clue in the
midst of what was purported to be a request for other
services. An act such as this demonstrates either
implicit trust or sheer desperation. Regardless of the
motivation, the student is seeking the counsel of a
wiser adult in a confidential relationship. It creates
an awesome situation for a counselor to provide such
vital help to a troubled student in his or her attempt
to achieve academically while undergoing racially-based
outside stress. Unfortunately, there is no quick-fix
for such problems that disturb the student's equilibrium
in the classroom. Counselors must then draw upon their
own moral and religious orientation to help clients
examine their own situations with clear eyes and form
their own decisions based on the known facts. The
counselor must not become judgmental at this point in
the relationship but rather should discard, or at least

rise above, racist rules or customs which foster the social separation of persons on the basis or color, race, or religion. (See: **"Managing Your Own Racism."**) In tense and developing situations, the counselor may be constricted by official local rules or customs but should not suggest the breaking of any law. As a change agent, counselors need to be in the forefront of student leadership and development in order to correct, promote and sustain healthy and friendly social activities among all students.

BLACK MIDDLE CLASS

Since the days of E. Franklin Frazier's <u>Black Bourgeoisie</u> (1962), in which this black social scientist based black middle-class designations chiefly on certain occupational groupings, there have been changes in who belongs and who does not. Dr. Robert Hill makes a relevant point in this regard in a recent article in Ebony (1987) by suggesting that the use of family income is a better indicator of class standing today. Citing the Tax Reform Act of 1986 passed by the U.S. Congress, Hill used it to set the definition of "middle class." Based on the Congressional classification of taxpayers in the Act, Hill said, ". . . we can now specify those who are not middle class. Households with incomes over $50,000 will be defined as 'upper class' while those with incomes between $10,000 and $20,000 are 'working class' and those with incomes under $10,000 are 'poor.'"

Using the 1984 U.S. Census, Dr. Hill further states that ". . . three out of ten (29 percent) black households are middle class, compared to almost half (44 percent) of white households. However, only 5 percent of black households are upper class . . . one fourth of blacks are working class, and two out of five black households are poor."

Once more, looking at the 1984 Census figures, less than half of middle-class blacks have attended college or completed a college education. There are indications that more are attending than ever before. The figures are probably indicative of the black affection for the "education is the way up and out syndrome."

Sometimes called the "backbone" of the black middle class, working couples earn a combined income to qualify for the classification. They are contrasted with their middle-class white counterparts where the male spouse either earns the entire income or the bulk of it. Generally, black wives work more frequently and earlier in the marriage than white wives and in lower-paying jobs as well. (See: "Culture and Social Class in the Black Community.")

EDUCATION AS A "WAY UP AND OUT"

Most of U.S. blacks live in metropolitan areas of the country today as contrasted with the rural life they lived earlier in the Twentieth Century. With the steady disappearance of the "American Family Farm," blacks moved to the city in hopes of finding better jobs and enriched lives for their families. Some were fortunate enough to secure good work opportunities and began the slow climb out of poverty and deprivation. Most rural blacks were not able to do so in the earlier years, thus creating a cycle of poverty which sociologists now call a "permanent underclass." Social planners are not very optimistic about breaking that cycle anytime in the foreseeable future. Significant changes in public policy will be needed to help turn the situation around.

About five years ago, I attended the first "Bynum, Harris, Medlock, and Parker Family Reunion" in a small Louisiana town where my parents were born and grew up. It was an event we all looked forward to with keen anticipation. About 150 family members attended. At the opening dinner, I was asked to give some remarks in response to my older cousin's historical, experiential review of the times, trials, and travails of blacks in that particular town. My advance family research indicated that among the adults in the combined families, nearly 100 percent had either some college or possessed one to three academic degrees. They are all presently engaged in productive occupations in many parts of the country. Those who have retired were previously employed in a variety of occupations and are still active contributors to their local communities.

My family had earnestly followed the path of education as the way out and upward into the higher reaches of society. Some of the youths present were currently in college studies at a variety of institutions of higher learning.

I recall in my early family life that my siblings and I were constantly told by our elders to "be somebody!" The aspirations and expectations were everpresent -- not only from parents, but from the extended family and adult friends. As one looks back on the growth years, it is clear that parental stress (I prefer to term it "encouragement") was necessary in order for us to achieve. This was all against a backdrop of segregation and racial discrimination which stripped away feelings of self-worth and legally denied equality of persons. In spite of these hurdles and restraining walls, many of my generation persisted and managed to achieve academically. Unfortunately, most could not. While I cannot claim that all black families value education so strongly, there are many who still adhere to the anonymous adage: "What you put into your head, no one can take away from you." That is still good advice today for anyone.

The age of the Eighties and Nineties provides excellent opportunities for increased community support for good education for blacks at all levels so that the masses can rise from the underclass position to which they have been relegated. Dr. James Comer (Ebony, 1987), an expert in child development at Yale University, has urged black community organizations to lead a crusade "at home and at school" to set realistic academic expectations for black children. He believes that the schools cannot do it all, but the facts of low economics and low social skills of many black parents make it difficult for them to give the encouragement and direction to young people as they grow up. Thus, Dr. Comer has called for a total involvement of the black community in the support of public education in this country. There can be no acceptance of second or third class schools for blacks or of the abandonment of public education in favor of private schools by proposed government subsidies such as the "tuition tax credit" or "education vouchers." From an economic standpoint alone, such approaches to education would virtually eliminate blacks from entering the "better" private schools. Only those few whose families are affluent enough would qualify.

An interesting and successful program devised by Dr. Comer through his work at both the Yale Child Study Center and some area inner-city public schools is "A Social Skills Curriculum for Inner-city Children." This program involved the parents, who themselves were poor and undereducated, in an attempt to reinforce the importance of their children learning basic skills. This was all coordinated with information on health, nutrition, economics, political awareness, and an appreciation of the arts. The special teaching of social skills in the classroom stimulated both the child and the parent and began to open up other horizons previously unknown to them. The program was so successful that the school district soon installed it in local middle schools and high schools.

The avenue of education as a way up and out should be provided for by all communities with full citizen support in order for schools to produce more well-educated blacks who will become contributors to life and not just public dependents and problems. This preventive approach should assist in building better communities in which all can live, work, and play while enjoying the differences in race or color.

FIVE

BLACK YOUTH IDENTITY
AND SELF—IMAGE

BLACK COMMUNITY STRUGGLE

There is a continuing battle in the metropolitan
black community between the role models of the
"subterraneans" (Blackwell 1975) and the "legitimates"
-- a sort of life and death tug of war between the
forces of evil and good. The prize in the contest is
the youthful mind and body. Each side attempts to
convince the youth that its style of life and growth is
the best. On the one hand, the subterranean group is
outside the law, dealing in narcotics, gambling, and
other vices which produce for it much illegal money
which is used in a flashly manner. This lifestyle has a
certain attraction for the unsophisticated black
youngster who can see with his own eyes, but only as far
as the money, fast and expensive cars, flashy clothes,
jewelry and sex. Because these "shadies" (Drake and
Cayton, 1962) and (Billingsley, 1968), are so prevalent
in the black neighborhoods, the impressionable children
look to them as role models. The honest lifestyle of
hard-working parents and other family members seem
humdrum and ordinary in comparison. In fact, the
"legitimates," who are the best "significant others,"
should provide the strongest influence over the child,
but the "shadies" render them almost powerless.

An observer might easily ask, "Why is this tolerated by the good people in the black community?" and "Are there not legal remedies and local police to correct these situations?" These are legitimate questions, but especially in the black community there is little or no history of the local justice system coming to the aid of citizens when black-on-black crime is being committed. Accordingly, black people find it hard to believe that there is as much interest by white officials in their problems as that which is apparent in white neighborhoods. Comer (1972) called the right to be liked a basic human need in that "needing to belong creates despair for a black man in a white-controlled, racist society." He further suggests that "black adults must feel that they are preparing their children for full and fair participation in society. They must feel that they belong, are valued, and have something to contribute to the society."

Through a variety of negative experiences in the neighborhood, at school, in the courtroom, and in the media, blacks see themselves as not only rejected, but perceived by whites as only a self-induced problem. Psychologists have said that humans usually react negatively to rejection either in a subtle or overt manner. Frequently the reaction is embodied in either apathy, alcohol and drug abuse, crime, or other deviant types of behavior. There is too much of such rejection and, hence, too much resultant anti-social behavior in the black community.

BLACK IDENTITY NEEDED

As one of the few white psychologists who recognized the need for a positive identity in black youth, Eric Erickson (1968) in Youth Identity spoke of "a developing identity" which needed fostering. He urged a "more inclusive identity" for blacks, if not total absorption and integration as Americans. Erickson further contended that a developing identity needs some "historical actualities" on which to count. What they are, he concluded, is the remaining question. Society cannot permit the arresting of the development of black youth into positive and productive members of the total community. In that regard, the wider society must make it possible for these young people to experience an equal chance for growth as individuals without the limiting stigma of color. The classic postulation of Cooley's (1922) "looking-glass self" comes alive when based on our own perceptions of the reactions of others. If one is consistently told or shown by negative remarks and acts that he is not a worthy person, then his self-concept will take on a lowered status. Confronted often enough with a negative self-concept, the individual will internalize its meaning and permit it to persist as a serious reinforcement of the perceived external judgments. That is a condition which most individuals cannot overcome by themselves, so they generally conform to, and, may tragically enough, become the perception.

In explaining the concept of "the significant something," Martin and Martin (1978) said it demands recognition. One's status in the family and perhaps in the community is often determined by what the person does well. It says he or she is "something" or "somebody." The action could be the playing of basketball, cooking, singing, deep knowledge of the Bible or any of a variety of simple or complex accomplishments. Conversely, the status of another person may also be high or low because of a negative "significant something." Thus, even a gossiper, or one who consumes large quantities of liquor, or an imaginative "cusser," or a flitting lovemaker may find himself or herself shunned by those who do not participate in such activities. It does not matter what one's socioeconomic status happens to be. The possessor of a positive "significant something" says he or she is an individual and is somebody in the eyes of the community. When students come to college as young adults, they bring along what Chickering (1969) said were "the stereotypes of masculinity and femininity in terms of which they have viewed themselves . . .(but later) yield to more complex views . . ." The emotional

load and impact of this area of identification is heavy
and important. It is not uncommon for a young black man
to arrive on campus with a "macho" image, hoping to
either impress or, perhaps, frighten others into
accepting his behavior as "right on." He may be street-
wise smart but probably not sophisticated or suave in
his manner. He soon discovers that the campus milieu is
quite different from his old neighborhood, but he
continues for some time in this style. This attitude
may even carry over into the classroom where he may be
met with resistance from professors who tolerate no
"heavies" in class. Unless the student is also
academically very bright and produces well in the
classroom, he may find himself fighting an uphill battle
in which the victor is always the professor. Socially,
the young man may succeed, but usually it is at the
expense of academic progress.

ACCEPTANCE DESIRED

By asking the question: "What do blacks think of
themselves?" the respected social scientific team of
Clark and Clark (1980) were able to report several
findings. Among these findings, and perhaps paramount,
was the desire of blacks to be accepted by all people
and in positive terms. The Clarks reported that blacks
have deep and persistent inner conflicts brought about
by the existence of racism in America. This condition
then gives rise to related ambivalences in their
struggle for a positive and personal self-image. To
protect themselves from racism, black people have had to
continuously resort to various, and sometimes very
sophisticated, evasive devices and coping mechanisms.
Among these mechanisms are: avoidance -- just trying not
to be in the vicinity where racism occurs; humor --
telling meaningless jokes or finding something funny in
each racist remark or action; and denial -- refusing to
buy into the racist moment by not acknowledging it as
such. All of these diversions might be called "the ways
of black folks" since they are employed on a daily basis
throughout the wider society. Relying on evasion to

protect one's own psychosocial structure often means the submersion of the true self-identity -- which can lead to more problems of personality and self-esteem.

TRUST LEVELS

Black youth try to find their rightful self-esteem in their own blackness but shy away from exposing their real emotions or gut feelings lest others misuse such deeply personal information. Counselors need to be aware of client reluctance for expressing openness and not feel that it is a deliberate attempt by the student to limit the relationship. The long and sorry institution of slavery (and later racial segregation) was the most effective method by which racist whites in the U.S. systematically denied blacks their humanness and, sometimes, their very lives. If, under the circumstances of slavery or segregation, a black person revealed much personal information, he or she often suffered at the hands of cruel whites because of it. The hard experiential lessons of slavery have been passed down through the oral tradition, from parent to child, with the admonition: "Don't tell all your guts to no white man." Since there is no real history of black persons being protected personally from harm by others, it is extremely difficult for young blacks today to trust whites who sit in positions of apparent or perceived, authority. It does not matter how sincere the white counselor is in the relationship, a statement of "you just have to trust me" goes nowhere with the young black person because he or she knows that there are other options available -- including: "No, I do not!" Frequently, the route chosen is avoidance -- that client will not likely reappear for advice from the same counselor.

As a youth growing up in Chicago's late twenties, the late celebrated author, Richard Wright (1977), described his reticence as a young black thrown into the wider society: "I hid my feelings and avoided all relationships with whites that might cause me to reveal them." The denial of feelings is perhaps one of the several causes of the alarming rate of hypertension in black persons nationwide. Therefore, counselors must be aware of the psychological danger for the black client and not mistake the denial or refusal to discuss feelings as though he or she has no current problems. In her autobiography, Singin' and Swingin' and Gettin' Merry Like Christmas, Maya Angelou (1976), wrote: "It wasn't wise to reveal one's real feelings to strangers. And nothing on earth was stranger to me than a friendly white." Feelings are considered by blacks to be closely guarded, personal property and anyone encroaching upon them is suspect. Even the standard counselor inquiry of: "Would you like to talk about it?" activates a built-in warning system which may actually reduce the level of trust, thereby putting the relationship in some jeopardy. This is not to say that all black students on predominantly white campuses will react in exactly this same way, but the majority will have some reticence about "opening up" and divulging their innermost secrets to a stranger. White counselors must first practice building a good relationship and establishing a trust level which will facilitate the student's academic and social progress.

NURTURING YOUTH

If young black students are to develop good self-images, there is the need for a supportive environment which nurtures and does not negate. Necessarily, a portion of that nurturing must come from the family unit or from some "significant other" who is a part of the student's life. Perhaps it is an observant teacher who encourages or a guidance counselor who points out a career possibility, or a friendly neighbor or adult friend who believes in the student's worth and urges him or her onward to become "somebody."

Many prominent black Americans have categorically stated that somewhere early in their lives there was this special person who made such an impression on their beings that they persisted in upward growth. Often the "mentor" did not know that their personal influence was significant in the development of many young black students who later achieved academically and in living. Good role models are necessary for black youths to emulate.

There seems to be an unspoken code between black men which requires that they speak to each other or make some physical sign of recognition even though they have never met before. This bond of black maleness as such may be misleading in that others who observe the exchange of greetings between black men may receive a stereotyping impression that "all blacks know each other." One can only speculate how and when the pleasant custom began. My own experiential explanation revolves around the black person's need to feel some form of recognition as a human being in a largely white society where he is often perceived of as "an invisible man" (Ellison, 1952). Black men are, in their own way, saying to each other: "I see you and recognize you as 'a brother.' You are a friendly face!" (But, black men do not like to hug each other!) On some predominantly white college campuses, another black face may be the only one that shares a smile, or other friendly greeting that day. That is most unfortunate -- not only for black persons, but also for whites who miss an opportunity to expand their own personal horizons when they ignore others from different cultures or races. The white counselor observing this "ritual" should understand it within the context of a hopeful people wishing to be not only alive, but human as well.

Black women are friendly to each other but in different ways from black men. This is due in part to the "programming" received in growing up. Not only do they pause to greet other black women but may even extend it to white women as well. In private social gatherings, black women are known to affectionately use the word "girl" while conversing with each other but never in front of whites. It would be quite demeaning and discounting for a white person to call a black adult female "girl" unless they are close friends. Blacks, like all other ethnic groups, prefer to be called by their own names. Counselors also should avoid giving a black student a nickname or using the diminutive form of his or her proper name. Students will tell you their preferred name if you will simply ask.

FAMILY STRENGTHS

Hill (1972), in Strengths of Black Families, reported five important factors found in black families: "adaptability of family roles, strong kinship bonds, strong work orientation, strong religious orientation and strong achievement orientation." These strengths have helped blacks to survive and advance in spite of great odds. They also have provided for greater stability in family units which had no binding glue provided by the wider society. Reviewing the further findings of the Hill study, it is evident that both egalitarian and matriarchal leadership exist in the black family. It is not singular (female-headed) as incorrectly presumed by Moynihan and his associates. The social mores of the 1980s appear to be causing all U.S. families to experience stress as demonstrated by the statistics which indicate a growing number of single parent families. There are many causes for this phenomenon among which is the high rate of divorce and the large number of teen pregnancies in which the teen's mother or grandmother keeps the child to rear.

Billingsley has stated: "For the Negro family, socialization is doubly challenging, for the family must teach its young members not only how to be human but how to be black in a white society. The requirements are not the same." Blacks historically have not shared with their white class counterparts a sense of "peoplehood." Their identities have been shaped, in great part, by the fact of slavery. Consequently, the American social system does not allow a common ground for equality. In a sense it is a foot race in which the white person is permitted to start first and the black person must follow but hop on one foot. It's not too difficult to predict the outcome.

SOCIAL CLASS DISTINCTION

When a counselor equates life-styles and automatically assumes that income is synonymous with class, he or she errs badly. Many persons of low income have middle-class values and desire a similar life-style, but the lack of money prohibits upward movement. Similarly, there are those middle and upper income persons who adhere to so-called lower-class values and life-styles. In modern America of the Sixties and Seventies, one observed a sweeping change in what was previously perceived to be a rigid, static and unmoving dividing line between the social classes. A period of "openness" helped to erase much of the tight class distinctions as it existed so that classes now overlap and cloud the categories. A word of caution -- social class still exists in both the white and black communities in America but chiefly based on the unreliable concept of family income. (See: **"Culture and Class in the Black Community."**)

For several generations blacks have equated high achievement with educational attainment. It is still felt in most of the black community that the key to upward mobility is education, which frequently means college and beyond. One serious problem with this view is the lack of adequate money in the black family budget to pay for all that education.

When a black youth from the neighborhood advances to the college level (especially one away from home), much is expected of him or her by family and friends. Because of the varied experiences on the college campus, these new students find themselves changing in ways that have a tendency to frighten even the strongest. They necessarily must become "different," and yet they have that strong wish to remain as they were before. They do not know that it is all right to have those feelings and that changes are going to occur if their continued educational experience does what it is supposed to do. Many such students find themselves allegorically "on the back of a tiger." They are afraid to stay on and too frightened to jump off. Black students, then, need special help if they are to make the transition from home to residence hall or from neighborhood to urban campus.

The understanding counselor, who is white, should look for ways to enhance the student's academic journey. A thorough knowledge of the black community's needs, desires, values and goals is an excellent way to start. Using such information relating to the social sciences of the group, a counselor can become that helper, that mentor, that quiet change-agent needed to effect student achievement. Patience and purposeful study will enhance the counselor's repertoire for helping students to succeed. (See: "Selected Reading List.")

Counselor recognition of the need for a good self-image on the part of students will produce equally good academic and social results which are essential and desirable for living a good life. It is a well-established fact that when one feels good about oneself, then that person is more likely to succeed at a high level of competence.

The counselor, who has the best interest of the client at heart, will carefully and consistently help students recognize personal "O.K." feelings, then assist them in building better positive self-images.

THE DISAPPEARING BLACK COLLEGIAN

William Raspberry, a syndicated newspaper columnist, recently wrote an article on "Blacks and Higher Education" in which he stated that much is happening to the black college student in the U.S. today. One of the most obvious situations in which youthful blacks find themselves is the serious lack of financial aid for college study. They are faced with the prospect of heavy loans which will later usurp too much of their earnings, once past graduation and into a job. This worries black students a lot. Another factor to consider is the increasing number of black men and women who are entering the military as an alternative to expensive higher education, perhaps delaying college until the tour of duty is over and a grateful government provides direct financial assistance. And, finally, Raspberry (1987) suggested by his research, that ". . . declining college attendance represents potential disaster for blacks. Low-skill entry-level jobs are rapidly disappearing, and young people without a college education are likely to find themselves on the economic scrapheap by the year 2000." The task is clear for counselors to encourage black clients to stay in college and graduate so that their chances of economic survival will be enhanced through the earning of a baccalaureate degree.

Wallace Terry (1984) wrote a best seller, Bloods, which detailed the Vietnam War as told by black veterans in their own words. The collected stories by Terry, a war-zone reporter for Time, were a chilling reminder of a "winless war" that cost the U.S. over 58,000 lives on the jungle battlefields, thousands of miles away from this country. Terry noted that black soldiers accounted for more than 23 percent of the fatalities in Vietnam, even though blacks were only about 10 percent of the total population in the U.S. This was a staggering loss of young men who would have been of college age had they lived. Their deaths, then, constituted a double tragedy in that young black women had fewer young men from which to choose mates. The loss of these men helped to create what might be called a generational gap in the establishment of black marriages and families. It can never be corrected.

The loss of black collegians to the campuses is being felt by many college officials who are currently planning and developing programs to retain and recruit more black students. If the college administrations are serious about improving their rates of retention, then many aspects of the problem need to be examined and improved. No single answer exists, but the potentially successful program will begin with a publicly proclaimed (and fiscally supported) commitment from the highest level of the college. Administrators will need to engender the cooperation and support of trustees, faculty, alumni, staff, and students in order for the program to be effective. Throughout the development of a recruitment and retention program, the local black community should be involved and kept informed of the progress. It is a tough problem which will require the assigning of high priority to the project by all those who have some responsibility for its being.

SIX

CULTURE and SOCIAL CLASS in the BLACK COMMUNITY

BLACK AMERICAN HISTORY LIVES

When Moynihan and Glazer (1963) called the Negro ". . . an American and nothing else . . .," they erred principally by discounting the values and culture of blacks and, in so doing, devalued an entire race of people. These two respected researchers seemed to believe that the entire history of Black Americans is non-existent. Such a negative view of a people deny them as a group their own humanity.

On the contrary, black Americans do have a long history, a distinguished heritage, important values, diverse goals and hopeful dreams. They have contributed substantially to "the making of America" as aptly described by Benjamin Quarles (1964) in his famous history of America's blacks and their struggle of more than three centuries for personal and group freedom as guaranteed by the U.S. Constitution. Quarles noted that blacks suffered through many decades of disappointment after the close of the bloody U.S. Civil War. Very little improvement for the vast majority of slavery's descendents was experienced in an entire lifetime.

Despite all the gloom and the denial of African and even the white man's culture, blacks labored for generations in the fields, factories, and shops. They acquitted themselves as patriots through the shedding of their blood and even loss of their lives in foreign lands, fighting wars they did not start. It would seem that such devotion to country and the work ethic would be enough to vouchsafe a comfortable place in the total American social, economic, and political structure. Unfortunately, it did not.

DUALISTIC SOCIETY

The racist atmosphere in cultural development and in all other important phases of living stymied the new black citizen from achieving his or her full potential. Blacks, therefore, have been forced to live and operate in a dual world, playing dual roles which have a divisional effect on personality development. In virtually all areas of the nation -- in towns, cities, and even in institutions of higher learning, there is currently a pluralistic society -- one side white, and the other side black. W.E.B. DuBois (1903) described the condition as "twoness -- an American, a Negro; two souls, two thoughts, two warring ideas in one dark body." There seems to be little activity to bring the two states of society into a harmonious single one where everyone has an equal chance to succeed and experience the "American Dream." Martin Luther King, Jr., the late civil rights activist, voiced this notion in his famous "I Have A Dream" speech in which he hoped for a world where people are judged by their characters rather than by their skin color. Fortunately, that hope is still alive throughout the country, and the message is being carried forward by people of goodwill who continue to believe that some significant changes can be made.

VALUE SYSTEMS CONTRASTED

It is important that counselors be aware of black culture and class structure within the context of the total society. Equally important is the necessity to recognize and appreciate the differences found in the culture (and subcultures) and to understand how it got that way. Some of the differences are significant and can be found in many areas of daily life. They are too numerous to list and describe in this book, but they include: church liturgies, food, fashion, personal interaction, names, speech, morals and values, use of money, work, and family.

With my development and teaching of a sociology course, "The Black Community," there has been an opportunity to contrast the two cultures so that one could recognize value differences in this manner: a) Blacks are more expressive and creative in their church liturgies by a vocal response to the preacher's "call" and participation in the singing of stirring music. White church liturgies are more reserved in tone and less open in terms of congregational involvement in the service; b) Blacks think of money as not being important in itself but in terms of what can it do and how it is used. Whites tend to use money to control and to save it for future use; c) Blacks think of the group as having primary importance. Whites depend upon individualism to make one's mark in society; d) Blacks prefer to look at personal qualities as the best guide for determining social status. Whites base status on income, race, family, even on religion and "maleness"; e) Black morality revolves around personal dignity and how you treat others. Whites look to God and personal behavior to structure a moderated moral basis for living; f) For blacks, time is relative -- the "now" is most important. Whites permit time to regulate their lives. "One must be punctual in order to be taken seriously." Usually, after the lecture on the above topic of value differences, there is a spirited student discussion in which each racial group attempts to mollify itself with "explanations." As the discussion continues and the students begin to listen to themselves talk, it becomes apparent to them that the categorical statements made in the lecture actually describe each group's action and, by class period's end, a calm recognition of a level of truth is found in each of the statements.

Now, of course, it is impossible for anyone to say that "all of the above" is true of each person in either

44

group, but, within the social scientist's methodological framework, one can generalize and develop a thesis. That differences exist in value constructs is well known, and those values are in constant flux, chiefly due to changes (or adjustments) to life-styles, economics, politics, and religious tenets.

"OLD" vs. "NEW" SOCIAL CLASS STANDINGS

By way of comparison, Billingsley (1968) and Blackwell (1975) suggested that there was an "old" versus the "new" society class standing found in the black community. The "old" consists mainly of elders today who developed their style of life through family contacts and family money gained as entrepreneurs. Most of the businesses were located in black neighborhoods and for other blacks -- often started because the white merchants refused to service black people in their stores. Many of the self-made black social leaders had limited advantages for higher education but valued learning so much that they would send their children off to college in anticipation of a return some day to join the family business. Throughout the South in particular there are numerous black family dynasties still existing that started in this manner.

The "new" arose from the advent of young black people (in the Sixties and Seventies) being prepared for well-paying executive positions through the affirmative action of industrial giants. Others rose to high economic levels as self-employed physicians and lawyers or as top athletes or entertainers. Important to note is that, even when combined, the two groups in upper society are a relatively small number -- less than ten percent of all blacks. Billingsley noted further that both the "new" and the "old" are included in his study because the money they have and use was earned in a legitimate manner. Consequently, the "shadies" or "subterraneans" do not fit the category of upper-class because their money is illegally gotten. (See: "A Look at the Modern American Black Family.")

DUAL SOCIAL CLASSES

If one compared the black community to the white community in terms of social class standings, it would be apparent that the two groups are different in many significant areas. For example, medical doctors in the white community are generally considered to be middle class unless distinguished by great discoveries or outstanding procedural techniques. In contrast, the black physician automatically is accorded the position of upper-class in the black community because, to reach that career, one must have high academic achievement to earn the title of "Doctor." Blacks demonstrate great pride in knowing high-ranking black professionals or having them as personal friends. They also are careful to use that title of "Doctor" when referring to, or introducing, the person to whites. It is a statement of group worth which proudly says: "We have important, learned people, too."

In his book Black Awareness: A Theology of Hope, Major J. Jones (1971) described the black man's plight in the U.S. as substantially being noticed only when some other, unrelated condition made it necessary or when, for political expediency, there was also a pure economic need to do so. One would like to hope that motivation to do what is right comes from a moral position within the action group. Too often this is not the case. Sub-rosa interests, which are less moral or ethical, most often will submerge the lonely voice of "independent conscience." Blacks remember the historic words of Abraham Lincoln who said in a reply to statements by Horace Greeley in 1862, "My paramount object in this struggle is to save the Union and is not either to save or destroy slavery. If I could save the Union without freeing any slave, I would do it; and if I could save it by freeing some and leaving others alone, I would also do that." That was the highly politicized approach by the President of the United States to the solution of slavery.

It would be an injustice to suggest that President Lincoln and many other whites had no compassion for

blacks and their slavery conditions, for indeed they did
work hard toward its elimination. Their names and deeds
are legion, both Northerners and Southerners, who felt
that the subjugation of one human being by another was
despicable and intolerable. It was notably through the
sustained efforts of anti-slavery groups and individuals
that slavery was finally abolished and supported by
strong laws which should prevent its happening again.

BLACK SELF-CONCEPT EXAMINED

   The black person's self-concept according to Jones
(1971) "is partly determined by factors associated with
poverty and low economic class status. However, being
black in white America has many implications for the ego
development of young black children that are not
inherent in other lower-class membership." The black
child, by reason of birth, is thus placed in a color-
regulated class or caste system which forces a negative
self-image upon him or her as "a natural outcome of such
a system." Further, Staples relates in Black Sociology
(1976) that blacks traditionally have been characterized
as having a low self-esteem because of having whites as
their sole reference group. Yet the cultural model
suggests that many blacks have a high self-esteem and
positive self-concept because they are based in their
own culture. Staples also lists three components of
black culture: 1) that which is derived from mainstream
America; 2) those from similarly oppressed peoples; and
3) that which is unique among Americans of African
descent. If an assumption is made that all three
components are placed in proper perspective and acted
upon, then positive self-concepts should develop in the
children of such a cultural situation. That in itself
is a very large requirement in order for blacks to
experience a level of self-esteem comparable to whites.
   When the black child develops in a color caste
system, he or she may assume the lower status prompted
by the existence of institutionalized racism found in
"de facto" segregated neighborhoods and schools. There
are few counteractive forces available to the average

black child which will reverse the psychological and
emotional feelings of low self-worth and will open the
avenues for high self-esteem. Thus, the black child may
very well learn self-hate and self-doubt early in life.
Counselors should be aware of this cultural phenomenon
and work with black clients to dispel such notions of
self-doubt as they relate to academic success. One of
the best approaches is to offer sincere and realistic
encouragement toward the student's educational goals,
using all the information and resources available. A
statement of "You can do anything . . ." is grossly
insufficient. It should be remembered that no matter
what one's goals are and how responsible one may be,
others in the social system need to be at least equally
responsible and willing for the reaching of those goals
to occur or for success to happen. Counselors should
constantly remind black students to "keep their eyes on
the prize," whatever that may be, then urge working
smarter and harder so that they may reach their goal
within an acceptable time.

MEASURES OF CLASS POSITION

As in all cultures, class positions are measured by
certain indicators easily recognized by the group. They
may differ from time to time, but the central thrust
will usually remain intact even though elements may
change. It is not an easy task to determine just why
one remains in the lower class of an open society.
Lower class persons are constantly aware of their
positions but usually do not know how to go about
improving that position for a variety of reasons. It is
the author's opinion that the theories about the lack of
ambition or innate happiness with a life of hardship are
at best unprovable. There are those in the social
science realm who argue that lower-class persons are
somehow "culturally deficient." That is, they do not
fully comprehend and cannot follow the norms set by
higher social classes. Unfortunately, many whites apply
that theory to all blacks, but it is plausible that
lower-class persons simply think the higher class norm

is not really relevant to their world and so they automatically reject it.

In most of the world where society is advanced beyond the rural, agricultural stage, the measures of occupation, wealth, property, family, religion, education, income, and residence are considered to be the highest measures of social class. No single measure is generally enough -- there are usually two or more indicators which help qualify a person or family for social ranking.

Depending on which theorist you choose, the social class strata in the U.S. can be defined in at least a dozen ways. Only four will be briefly described here: 1) Three class theory. This is the most popular approach and is sometimes considered the simplest. It includes lower class, middle class, and upper class. 2) Six class theory. It divides the three classes into lower-lower, upper-lower; lower-middle, upper-middle; lower-upper, upper-upper. 3) Five class theory. This arrangement repeats the six class theory but has only one upper class. 4) Occupation level theory. An example of this theory is the Lynds' ranking of "Middletown" (Muncie, Indiana) by the terms "working class" and "business class," or by "blue collar" and "white collar." All the above rankings appear to depend upon two factors: the relative complexity of the social system under study and the data gathered as a base.

Since most of the black community does not rate high in income earned and occupations, the "Style of Life" measure appears to be the most valid manner of determining class position. My rationale for advancing this approach is that it embodies some logic. It has been demonstrated that social intimacy occurs when people (of any color or race) consider others as comparative equals. An additional aid in the process is the possession and use of certain consumer items which set the different social classes apart. Thus, "Style of Life" can be observed, tabulated, and evaluated either informally or formally by group persons or researchers.

Social intimacy is measured in the black community by examples such as: membership in certain churches, lodges, fraternities, social and pleasure clubs; or by: one's speech patterns, auto driven, residence, electronic gadgets, wearing apparel, and type of pleasure travel. Possession of a higher education degree which includes a title of "Doctor," or an occupation which calls for the use of "Professor," will usually ascribe to that individual a high level of social status. While this measure of class position is comprehensive and is thus an advantage, one of its serious drawbacks is the temporary nature of the significance of consumer items as status symbols, and that personal recreational interaction does not always follow strict class lines. It is possible for the lines to merge or be crossed at will when mass production brings the treasured consumer items within the grasp of persons in a lower economic status.

The significance of social class is approximately the same in the black community as it is in the white community -- it is often directly related to such things as delinquency rates, crime rates, divorce rates, school drop-out rates and personality disorders. Social class differences have significance in attitude and value orientations. Persons in a particular perceived social rank usually will have certain expectations of life and its opportunities. They will generally view social reforms and feelings about education, religion, and other aspects of social life differently from persons of other social ranks. Social class has great significance for intimate social participation. Whether one attends a classical music concert; goes to hear a pop singer travels to Europe for the summer, or visits a shopping center parking-lot carnival midway depends on the individual's perception of his or her own class position. Even these measures will get muddied by crossover in the black community, thus erasing the perception of rigid class lines. Perhaps the only universal or classification statement that can be safely made is that one's _first_ position in the social order is determined by the social class his immediate family occupies. This obtains regardless of the individual's personal attributes or potential.

SEVEN

RACISM, STEREOTYPES AND PREJUDICE

U.S. RACISM AND RACIAL DISCRIMINATION

Oliver Cox (1948) stated categorically that "...the world did not practice racism until after Columbus discovered America." This brilliant sociologist concluded that racism came about as a part of the system used to exploit blacks into slave labor. Eventually, it was supported and justified by color of skin not by nationality or conquered people alone.

In 1968 the "Kerner Report" issued the stinging statement: "Our nation is moving toward two societies, one black, one white -- separate and unequal." This was no great revelation to black people. Nonetheless, it was at last a public, government-supported admission of the racist character of the dominant society. The Kerner Commission, composed of distinguished Americans, studied race relations in the U.S. at the request of then-President Lyndon B. Johnson for several months and concluded with a far-reaching report on racism and its evils. It was hoped by black and by sympathetic white Americans that the publication of this data would precipitate a welcome change in America's oppressive prevalent social system. After two decades of opportunity, the change has been interminably slow.

Frequently an escape mechanism is employed to disguise racism or to apologize for racist behavior that is to casually dismiss the offending party as "sick" or mentally ill. On the contrary, the "sickness" of racism pervades the dominant society -- all kinds of persons are racist. The mental illness explanation is only one form of compensation and is not acceptable from either a logical or moral point of view. Dollard (1937), a noted social scientist, in his Caste and Class in a Southern Town identified three specific "gains" accruing to whites as a result of black oppression. They are: economic, sexual and prestige. The whites who pursue any or all of these "gains" were under the protection of bad laws and practically guaranteed success. In Racism and Psychiatry, Thomas, et al. (1972) declared: "In our society, racist acts are so institutionalized that they can be indulged in as a matter of course by persons who are not pathological." Such ingrained, deeply rooted racism sustains the white group's authority over the lives of black people who finally lose hope of growing into whole, responsible, contributing persons in society.

When racist persons wish to discriminate against a group of a different color or race, they usually develop a series of tactics which exclude the out group. The exclusion is justified or rationalized by pointing out certain racial ideologies which designate the out group as being naturally inferior. To strengthen their argument, racists insist that the out minority deserves the less-than-equal treatment on the basis of a false ideological concept of "natural inferiority." U.S. (white) society rationalized black slavery in this manner for nearly three hundred years and, for a hundred-plus more, justified racial segregation and discrimination of black people.

The number of racial myths is legion. These are useful to the racist as reasons to deny the humanity of a large group of people. They do not, of course, bear up under scientific and humanistic scrutiny even though some were deemed "scientific" by persons who are not scientists themselves. A few of the earliest myths frequently used to maintain the ideology of slavery were:

1) Blacks were uniquely fitted for bondage.
2) Blacks were prone to insanity in "unnatural" conditions.
3) "Faithful" slaves were happy-go-lucky.
4) The Negro brain was smaller and less developed for creativity than whites.
5) Blacks were incapable of being educated.

It is sad to relate that after more than a hundred years following the Emancipation Proclamation, which freed the slaves, some of these myths are not dead but crop up in present day society. Current popular racial stereotyping by whites of blacks includes statements about "natural rhythm, athletic ability, and sexual superiority (by both sexes)" (Grier and Cobbs 1968). The inference is that there can be nothing in their heads but muscle, mush, or depraved desires. Blacks and others of goodwill spend an inordinate amount of time and energy trying to challenge and change the behavior of racially prejudiced people. This is an ongoing battle requiring vigilance and determination to safeguard the rights of all Americans.

Thirty years have passed since the U.S. Congress voted into law the Civil Rights Act which created the U.S. Commission on Civil Rights and a Civil Rights Division in the Justice Department. These agencies were believed necessary to protect and insure the rights of all persons under the U.S. Constitution. Their life and activities have been stormy but, in some ways, seemed productive for blacks. While "anti-black" laws have been repealed or set aside by courts, there are some locales where the condition of custom and tradition (held by whites) tends to overshadow law and moral right. This fact alone gives validity to the establishment and continuance of U.S. government agencies charged with the responsibility to see that equality of opportunity exists at all levels in the country. The narrowly defined political issue of "States Rights" is necessarily diminished in order to guarantee the civil rights of individuals and to punish those who would illegally deny those rights. In recent years there have been efforts by opponents of equality of opportunity to the continuance of the Civil Rights Commission by insisting that the need no longer exists because everyone is now equal. Counselors should know that the current facts in this matter do not support the idea that "all is well" in America. The contrary is true. We are in deep trouble when it comes to race relations, employment, police protection, political representation, education, and social services to the poor. Knowing the depth of the current conditions through his or her own searching for information will keep the counselor aware of the damage being done to the black clients' emotional, social, economic, physical and psychological selves.

HISTORIC PREJUDICE

Allport (1958) spoke of "The Principle of Least Effort" as the premise used frequently by prejudiced people who desire simplicity in their faulty reasoning. Following this rule-of-thumb, the prejudiced person can fit people into neat boxes with a single stereotype or other erroneous belief about the targeted group. In addition, an affected person may select and explain so-called "evidence" according to that person's own particular bias. Consequently, it is devastating to all parties concerned when "cause and effect thinking" is employed in such situations -- once more to simplify -- creating causation when there is none.

As a result of historic prejudice on the part of whites, black people have tended to develop a repertoire of defense mechanisms -- sometimes referred to as "ego defenses." Among Gordon Allport's listing of mechanisms are: denial of membership in the attacked group, obsessive concern, withdrawal and passivity, passive acquiescence, clowning, shyness and cunning, aggression against own group, sympathy, fighting back (militancy), and enhanced striving. There are many other examples not so neatly catalogued, but they serve as coping devices among those who feel the stress of prejudice in their lives. For example, blacks will, among themselves, frequently turn this labeling around and make something positive out of it -- sometimes in great humor. That way it "saves face" in an attempt to remain a whole person in a demeaning society. More often though, blacks tend to succumb to the repeated suggestion of low worth and behave accordingly -- much to their own chagrin.

The dynamics of cognition in the prejudiced person tend to give rise to generalizations and often to double-value judgments. Such a person prefers simple categorizations and is very much resistant to personal change and even admits that his or her theory is a "little weak," but clings to it anyway. Being bothered with the facts is burdensome and not very useful to the prejudiced individual.

Counselors should be wary of labeling students; even in the privacy of their own minds on the basis of personal biases or beliefs. The overall effect of such acts is to destroy the relationship, the trust, and the client's own ego and self-worth. Many white persons who have little positive contact with blacks tend to slip into a racist pattern without recognizing it -- and will justify such behavior when confronted by saying "everyone calls them that . . ." or "It's what I've always heard."

A MATTER OF CONSCIOUSNESS

The fact of race and the knowledge of other races or skin colors is always a matter of consciousness. Such consciousness can lead to racial prejudice. The prejudiced person simply prejudges with internalized negative feelings toward a group to which he or she does not belong. Some prejudices derive from direct experiences which were "bad" in social terms. Most prejudices are taught -- usually by example -- to little children in their formative years by members of the primary group to which they belong. These prejudices are usually at a high emotional level which encourages an aversion to all members of the despised group. During the Seventies and Eighties, it has not been unusual to see a tableau on the television evening news which permitted a white parent to prompt his own preschool child to verbalize parent-taught epithets against blacks or other minority groups. The child obviously did not understand the serious nature of this act but performed it at the behest of the father who bitterly denounced all people not like himself. A demonstration of prejudice such as that should bring to mind a phrase from the timeless musical, "South Pacific," which admonished the prejudice-troubled heroine: "You've got to be taught to hate, before you are six, seven, or eight. . ." It clearly defines, in childlike terms, how prejudice begins. Life is not, unfortunately, like a well-written story to which a happy ending can be added at will. Can you imagine how little black children who view racist acts in the media must feel when subjected to such an attack? What would you as the black parent say to your child at a time like that? The hurt experienced by the black family watching the display is doubly devastating -- first, because the very act was undeserved, and, second, by the frustration of not being able to do anything about it.

There are, however, some positive prejudices which are considered as worthwhile sentiments such as: pride, patriotism, and loyalty. Negative prejudice is a "bad" thought or act because it elicits a behavior based on something other than good and it is against someone or some group unlike oneself.

Human children are great imitators -- that is how we learn most of what we know by age seven or eight. We watch our older siblings, parents, extended family adults, neighbors, friends, TV personalities, and others, then mimic when the time comes to express a feeling or an attitude. Much of our early attitudinal formation remains with us into adulthood, thus shaping our behavior towards others. If an early attitude (and resultant behavior) is negative in connotation, it may never be changed without conscious, serious desire and hard work to make it happen. The counselor who is aware of the "sickness" of racism in him self or herself and discovers the need to change is, indeed, fortunate, for there are ways of overcoming it. (See: **"Counselor Behavior and Client Relationships."**)

DAMAGING STEREOTYPES

The stereotyping of all blacks (in whatever manner) can lead to what Ginzberg (1967) called "serious error in the design and implementation of policies aimed at eliminating segregation and discrimination." It would behoove all social planners and interactors to realize that blacks are as different as any other racial or ethnic group when one looks at individuals and not at the simple matter of skin color identification.

DeFleur et al. (1973) clearly defined stereotypes as "clusters of beliefs that are uniformly applied to certain groups of people." These beliefs, or statements, are prejudicial toward the group in question when they are in the negative sense. So, when anyone refers to blacks as having rhythm, being happy-go-lucky or lazy, or ignorant, he or she is perpetuating an unrealistic set of conceptions. Since this set of human traits is not uniformly true of any group, then such statements should not be used. Stereotypes, whether voiced or thought, serve only to damage the image of the group under attack. Unfortunately, the entertainment field (notably the Hollywood movies) has supported the stereotyped black person for many years. Only lately has there been any movement in the direction of telling a film story with "real black people" in it who live, talk, and react like others in the society.

However they may be used, DeFleur states that stereotypes ". . . are stinging insults to the minority groups that are the victims of the antipathies they express. At the same time, they are techniques for maintaining prejudice at the personal level." In the U.S. stereotypes have become a part of the wider culture because they are so commonly shared, believed, and verbalized. They have become, through usage, a part of the folkways of society that get passed on from generation to generation principally through the oral tradition.

Counselors guilty of stereotyping by belief or by actual verbalization need to concentrate on a self-study of black social sciences and consider serious personal change before continuing to counsel black clients. A strong internal signal of counselor racial bias is sounded if, while reading this book, the white counselor feels angry enough to "compensate" for, or try to rationalize, his or her own negative racial attitudes with irrational explanations. To recognize and deal positively in an effective manner with such deep personal feelings requires intellectual honesty and a good measure of individual integrity. (See: **Managing Your Own Racism.**")

DENIAL OF COLOR

In Racism and Psychiatry, Sillen and associates (1972) suggest that the defense of "colorblindness" in race relations is an "illusion" if it means the denial of differences in the experience -- in the culture and psychology of black Americans and other Americans. Counselors (and other helping persons) need to see the skin color difference, appreciate it, and understand what the needs of the client happen to be -- but based on sound knowledge. That knowledge should include information about the black student's culture, history, deprivation, life-style, yearnings, goals and ambitions. Blacks are not "collective children." Rather, they are individuals belonging to a societal outgroup desiring full personal freedom. Sillen further suggests that errors are made in some studies of the black personality when the researcher ignores the individual and intensity of reactions to the stress of living as a nonvalued person in a racist society. Most studies are done in terms of black pathology with a simplified desire to place all blacks into a single "basic personality." Valuable data is left unused when researchers ignore all that is healthy and good in a group's life. Additionally, much of the research on blacks has been done using very small samples, such as twenty-five patients, in The Mark of Oppression by Kardiner and Ovesey in 1951. Certainly, most professional counselors are aware that the foundations of Freudian psychiatry were developed on the weight of only _five_ published cases! It would appear that such research was not performed according to the scientific method which requires more data and has been the standard of investigations even in the realm of the "hard sciences." It becomes purely pathological in content including a denial of any creativity or positive forces or action and so condemns the group to utter helplessness.

"Harlem," a poem by the celebrated Langston Hughes (1959) discusses the "deferred dreams" of black folk by posing in literary style these questions: do they dry out and become something less, or smell like decaying matter, or become unbearable burdens, or do they fight containment until there is final self-destruction? It is probable that all of the above are experienced by black people at some time in their lives. When blacks observe the obvious joy afforded by immediate gratification which most whites naturally expect from society, then they know that everything is not equal for everybody. Consequently, the high level of frustration felt by black students greatly usurps the emotional and physical energy necessary for academic success. Certainly, the individual counselor cannot right all perceived wrongs, but he or she can be understanding and assist the black student in coping with negative situations in a nondestructive manner.

The American society and its educational system are both harborers of prejudice. Attitudes which emanate out of the institutionalized system of prejudice found in the culture are sometimes viewed as products of a group phenomenon, not just the thoughts of an individual. Prejudice then becomes a part of the folkways and other norms which are validated for future generations through the human socialization process. Counselors are called upon to help break the line of prejudice and provide a liberating atmosphere at least within one's own office to promote the development of good relationships and, hopefully, steady progress toward academic success.

EIGHT

BLACK STUDENTS ON WHITE CAMPUSES

REALISTIC GUIDANCE NEEDED

It is imperative that counselors realize that the largest number of black college students come from the working poor families of the nation. By all applicable standards, only a small percentage of the black community can be considered middle class. It is often estimated at 17-23 percent. Yet, as the black student achieves in college, he or she generally is accorded middle-class status by friends and family in the black community (Ginzberg, 1967). (See: **"A Look at the Modern American Black Family."**)

As a social scientist and as an educator, the author believes it is necessary that young black students receive help in self-image development, not only from their families, but from education personnel who are in frequent contact on a teaching/guidance level. Many excellent opportunities exist in the educational setting for realistic guidance and career advising to be done. Black students repeatedly have felt they needed more realistic guidance in the areas of prerequisites for career objectives and orientation towards college and other post-secondary schools (Ginzberg, 1967). Ginzberg further suggests that student "practice" on psychometric instruments at the high school level is important for the transition to college. It is through such academic activities that black students will learn their aptitudes and begin to make reasonable career choices. If uncaring school personnel or institutional racism denies them the chance to learn in this way, black students will suffer much. They will most likely be automatically tracked into low-level, non-collegiate studies. The knowledgeable high school counselor who understands black student needs and wishes to help them grow will urge them to take the SAT or ACT and any other similar achievement tests so they, too, can become competitive with their white cohorts.

A charge has been made against educators throughout the nation that they believe blacks cannot learn, so there is not much of an attempt to teach them. Wherever and whenever that attitude prevails, black students are robbed of their right to share the same opportunities as white students. To address this problem in education, perhaps a different classroom methodology might be necessary to interest a so-called "unteachable" student. There are theories and studies in the literature that address this question but without a generally accepted solution, either by the high school or ny the college.

Self-expression and assertion by youthful black students are necessary elements to achieve one's goals, according to black psychiatrist, Dr. Alvin Pouissant (1977). To exercise their rights, then, blacks must have a greater sense of control over their lives as do whites. Ergo, one must have charge of his or her own life in order to succeed.

Ten years after the 1954 U.S. Supreme Court decision, Brown vs. Board of Education of Topeka, the author had the opportunity to make some comments on the issue of school integration in The Hoosier Schoolmaster, a Midwestern education periodical (Bynum, 1964). Encouraged by great hope and trust in the American Creed, I flatly asserted that ". . . integration is a fact!" and went on to suggest that counseling was the key to survival of black students throughout the land. After more than three decades of slow and often painful progress, I believe that concept is still appropriate but needs to be clearly articulated for all students everywhere. It should be applied to the conduct of school boards, teachers, college trustees, state legislators, the U.S. Congress and general citizens. In addition, there is much that students from each racial group can learn culturally from the other while receiving a good education in a nurturing atmosphere of peace and goodwill.

COUNSELOR RESOURCES

The informed counselor must have a readily available reference and resource list of both on- and off-campus sources. This list should include not only alternative educational opportunities, but those services needed for daily living, for emotional or physical health, for financial assistance, emergency housing, and sources of other types of help. Of course it is important to have names to go along with the telephone numbers as well as addresses and other pertinent data for quick use. Keeping this list up to date is vital if it is to be of good use. To assure the validity of and the extent of the resources available, counselors should personally contact the references prior to including them in the list. Good starting points for finding sources in the black community are: the local branches of the Urban League, NAACP, YMCA YWCA, black churches and social organizations. These agencies and institutions will be pleased to cooperate when they learn that the counselor recognizes black students' needs both inside and outside the educational setting. Learning about their services will give the counselor confidence in recommending students as well as improving his or her credibility with the client. With good data in hand, you can tell a student what to expect from a source and, hopefully, reduce anxieties while motivating him or her towards personal action. (See: **"Community Resource List."**)

Black students are in some ways no different from other students -- they want counselors available to them but will sometimes overlook the counselor's need to have a life of his or her own. Counselors should be available, but with reasonable timing. Encourage office

62

visits by appointment and urge being on time so that
their tardiness will not encroach upon the next
student's time with you. There will always be the need
to make exceptions for true student emergencies such as
home problems, illness, and even car problems. Being
frank and honest with students can go a long way toward
the proper use of yourself as a helping person on
campus. It is a matter of personal preference whether a
counselor permits phone calls at his or her home. While
you wish to respond to the client and his or her needs,
your privacy should be of equal concern and not
constantly invaded. As the counselor provides
professional service within the bounds of a friendly
atmosphere and sincerity, care must be taken so one does
not become the client's buddy. Close fraternization
with students may prove to be a serious deterrent to a
good and lasting counseling relationship. Remain good
friends with clients within the context of helping them
toward academic success.

NEW ON CAMPUS

Many times a black student will arrive on a white
campus to begin studies and not receive any kind of
welcome from either white students, faculty or staff.
In those instances, the campus atmosphere begins with
negative behavior instead of a positive, pleasant
relationship. The student may feel like being put into
a "revolving door" which can sweep him or her out
quickly for an unscheduled return to the neighborhood.
More often than not, the student who returns home
unexpectedly suffers great embarrassment as old friends
and relatives will know he or she "did not make it in
college." Such a student unfairly begins college with
one foot tied to the other while other students have the
freedom of both feet to travel the long journey to
graduation day. Counselors who are aware will find a
way to become a part of the "welcoming committee" at the
beginning of the academic term so that black students
will feel that they, too, have a chance to succeed. The
time and energy put into such activities will bear fruit

later for counselor and student when an advising relationship develops.

Stikes (1984) raises another set of issues when he states that the black community and the black faculty and staff on campus all have a strong effect on the black students. In fact, Stikes believes that the black students are perceived by the black community as "positive" but the white university community sees them as "disadvantaged." Various coping strategies of black students may be strongly supported by the positive reinforcement provided by interested black faculty. Visible blacks in positions of authority generally are viewed by black students as valuable to their own survival. While a black administrator or faculty member is not expected to change the rules in favor of black students, at least there is the student feeling that fairness will exist. In a similar manner, some black students will retreat to on-campus black studies programs to improve their own self-identity and hopefully serve the black community after graduation. The ideal is to have the basic college curriculum infused with the black experience through particular courses, inclusion within standard course content, positive treatment in textbooks and equal treatment in the classroom. Unfortunately, very few colleges have attempted to follow that advice.

When black students appear to gather on campus and form little groups on their own, whites have a tendency to rationalize that "they segregate themselves." For some black students, this inward retreat may serve to suppress their individual social growth rather than help it expand. Black students experience an aloneness mostly because their white counterparts in general do not seek them out for friendship or as a source of information relative to academic study. One might argue that this condition persists because the white students generally come from families and neighborhoods that have little or no contact with black people except as service persons or they may simply view all blacks as "problems." Without some special effort being made, these home, family and neighborhood behaviors will continue misperceptions that are damaging. A counselor could become a catalyst by exploring and then, perhaps, facilitating opportunities for both racial groups to get together. Black and white students should be encouraged to participate together in athletic, theater, music, debate, language, art, science, dance, and other group activities. The important point is to have people interact naturally in a cooperative, social manner. Such activities, while promoting understanding and goodwill, should be helpful in the achievement of the ultimate goal -- attaining a higher education.

During the latter part of the year 1986 and the early part of 1987, there have been numerous media accounts of increased overt racism on college campuses particularly in the East and the North. Some of the disturbances have ended in a physical confrontation of black and white students during which some get hurt. College presidents and other administrators are rightly indignant over the use of racial epithets, slurs, and cross-burnings on campus. It appears that some white youths on some college campuses, feel it is acceptable to openly express hostile racial feelings in the educational setting. This should not become acceptable or overlooked by campus authority or local law enforcement officials. It also seems obvious from newspaper and television news that the level of anti-black feelings in the U.S. during the Eighties has risen concurrently with the activities of some high government officials who have tried to dismantle affirmative action and to change the federal judiciary to an ultra-conservative body. All of these conditions mitigate against the success of blacks in higher education as well as in other aspects of life.

In a keynote address to the National Academic Advisors Association in 1987, Dr. Jacqueline Fleming of Barnard College stated that "leadership skill is an effective antidote to the problems that black students face on white college campuses." She went on to say that black students usually have difficulty in finding outlets for their "achievement motivation." The correlates of such motivation are: fear of failure, fear

of success, and need for personal achievement. Blacks
so hampered, she said, ". . . are seriously frustrated
to the point of exhaustion and undergo the painful
experience of failure." Dr. Fleming's thesis is based
on her seven-year research project (funded by Carnegie
Foundation) <u>Blacks</u> <u>in</u> <u>College</u> (1984). She said that the
data indicated many black students find it difficult to
get positive attention from the classroom professor.
They tend to report that teachers are less interested in
them as students and show unfairness in grading. They
are thus unable to form warm, informal relationships
with the professors but rather are doomed to experience
cold and distant feelings in the classroom.

Giving a formula for solving the problems blacks find
on white campuses, Dr. Fleming suggested this solution:
"They are going to have to learn how to take control of
their educational experiences." They should, she
argues, learn how to do this by being more assertive,
not just aggressive. The desired assertiveness may be
best expressed through assuming the role of a leader on
campus. Following this theme, she concluded; "The
leadership role works because it maximizes all of the
relationships that are so critical to intellectual
development." Because leaders meet more people and thus
make more friends on campus, they attract the attention
of the faculty and staff who might become mentors, or at
least recognize them for their academic abilities in the
classroom. Leadership skill training is also important
to black students so that "dealing with difficult people
becomes less stressful and may culminate in the feeling
of effective control." Hopefully, the student will be
able to balance the outside classroom activities with
the academics and survive through graduation. The
counselor can assist the student's progress through this
process with friendly encouragement and perhaps tutorial
help when needed. It seems that a warm relationship
with an adult on campus is crucial to black freshmen as
they appear in what may be a very strange and unfriendly
place. If you can personally provide that needed "warm,
adult person" and some of the leadership skill training,
your services will be maximized and well appreciated by
both your clients and the college.

MIDDLE CLASS BLACK STUDENTS

Each college campus should at some time experience the enrollment of students from black middle-class families who will demonstrate many of the desirable characteristics of the wider society. They and their families generally have high academic achievement goals and, more than likely, will bring to campus a higher level of social sophistication and solid pre-college backgrounds. Therefore, it is the counselor's responsibility to know the student background before choosing a level of relationship. Middle-class black students know well the family's expectations of them and will strive to become as integrated into the campus structure as they are allowed. Most will not be first generation college persons -- their parents or siblings usually will have at least some college education or hold advanced degrees. It is not uncommon for middle-class black families to send their children to private secondary schools "in order to get a better education." Generally, middle-class students from a black family will have served as a community volunteer during high school as an expected part of the family's civic responsibility. Their families will have travelled on vacations throughout the U.S. and often abroad. The student usually accompanies the parents on these trips and participates in the learning process and vicarious horizon expansion which is a byproduct of pleasure travel. It is also assumed by the parents of the student that each child will go to college, begin a career, marry well and become a leader in the local community. Unfortunately, all of the children from middle-class families will not survive post-secondary educational experiences due to individual differences and choices. It is still the responsibility of the counselor to serve these highly motivated students so that they, too, can survive and graduate.

FINANCIAL AID

One of the most important factors in the facilitation of black students' persistence in college is the availability of financial aid information and the eventual receipt of funds. Most colleges and universities have specific persons or departments designated as specialists in financial aid information. This fact does not excuse the counselor from gathering all the data he or she can pertaining to scholarships, work study, loans and grants. If referrals are in order because of the institution's structure, the counselor should learn not only to which offices students should be referred, but also the person to see.

According to Astin (1982), "Work Study programs appear to facilitate student persistence, provided that the work is part-time (less than twenty hours per week) and (preferably) located on campus. Working more than twenty hours per week negatively influences undergraduate persistence, especially if the work is off-campus." Recent research indicates that black students who must work at a job outside the college setting are more likely to continue and reach the baccalaureate degree goal (Astin, 1982). Loans are not considered to enhance persistence, but scholarships and grants that are renewable based on realistic grade point average, do produce a pattern of continuance.

Financial aid packages which include some each of grant, work study and loan mathematically tend to equalize responsibility for loan payback and may also serve to reward academic diligence at the same time. Programs differ greatly from campus to campus and from fiscal year to fiscal year, depending on the availability of funds from all sources. Thus, it is necessary for the counselor to keep abreast of all the changes in the financial aid program and deliver that information in clear terms to the students and their parents or spouses. It may also be necessary to hold workshops or training sessions to assist students and parents in the filling out of the many financial aid forms. Activities such as these may additionally draw upon counselor time after regular office hours and may take place either on or off campus. Your help as a counselor certainly will be appreciated and will assist in the building of solid interpersonal relationships with students and their families.

SPECIAL DEVELOPMENTAL CAMPUS SERVICES

As black students arrive on your campus, what kinds of additional services are available to make the transition smoother for them and to assist in their continuance? Some colleges have recognized this as a vital need and provide a number of added helpful services to which black students are directed. Such services may become the "glue" which holds the black student and higher education together long enough for completion of a program of study. The services may be voluntarily staffed or may require dedicated college fiscal and human resources to operate effectively. Quite often there is a combination of the above methods of structuring the services. At the time of writing the first edition of this book, it appeared very unwise to depend upon outside funding such as federal government program money for support. Such was still the case at the time of the second edition. Extraordinary funds are scarce and generally are more difficult to find. Some colleges find it necessary to employ a special person or entire department for the sole purpose of developing such funds on a regular basis.

If your campus has no or few extra services for the black students in attendance, perhaps in your role as a change agent you may be able to spearhead the development. On campuses with a well-developed Department of Student Services, it may be possible to encourage the director of that unit to consider and install the needed services. You, as a counselor, should be able to use all your persuasive arguments to convince "the-powers-that-be" that young people deserve what you propose.

In the event that you are unable to find the resources needed to perform the above services, then it may become necessary to develop a voluntary "pilot plan" which should get some positive things started on campus. Quite often it is the small pilot program that receives attention because of its success that gets it funded later by the college. It is essential that the services be performed on campus so that it becomes an integrated, holistic program. The successful nation-wide programs in this area of academic development are in fact best when woven into the academic support services offered to all students. The writer, and no doubt many readers, are personally familiar with successful programs on well-known campuses throughout the U.S. Over the past decade the literature has chronicled and supported these programs as having positive impact on the problem of developing disadvantaged young people to their full academic and social potential. These campuses include the author's own, where he has had the opportunity to administer such a program for nearly a dozen years. Services like these will advance students toward their academic goals within the nurturing confines of an educational facility.

SUPPLEMENTARY SERVICES IDEAS

A suggested list of typical supplementary services and educational assistance for black students on campus will include, but should not be limited to, those below. Your own student-determined needs should be of the highest priority.

<u>Personal</u> <u>Reference</u> <u>Library</u>: Each student should be encouraged to possess several books to help in studying and writing papers while in college. The basic reference aids are listed below, but there are others the counselor can suggest which should be added as the student's money permits:

-A collegiate level, hard cover dictionary.
-A dictionary-form thesaurus.
-A writing-style manual or guide for writing term
  papers recommended by the campus English
  Department.
-A copy of a "<u>How-To-Study-In-College</u>" book.

If the student is hard-pressed for book money, remind him or her that all these books exist in the college library and could be used there until needed funds become available. Sometimes I have "desk copies" of certain texts given to me by publishers or by faculty colleagues which I loan to students in need. You may want to consider this too.

Tutoring: The educational literature is full of data relating to the general need for enhanced mathematical skills by black students. Astin (1982) reported a negative relationship of remedial mathematics needed by blacks to the three academic outcomes of undergraduate grades, undergraduate persistence, and completion of a graduate degree. A tutoring service could be set up in the campus library or other quiet location with peer-tutors screened by the appropriate academic department. In some colleges, it may be possible to convince the department itself to provide the tutors from its faculty or Teaching Assistants corps. Other areas of tutoring may include: reading, the sciences, and communications.

Study Skills: Some of the need in this important area may be satisfied by the issuance of a descriptive "do-it-yourself" book which allows the student to make improvement on his or her own time. A second level of help may be in the form of a short-term workshop scheduled prior to the beginning of classes or as a part of the "Freshman Summer Experience." An intensive, but longer, structured freshman orientation course may be indicated for certain residential campuses as the third approach to help the student settle down and begin the school year with greater confidence and efficiency.

Communication Skills: Most college English Departments are already aware of the lack of writing skills that all freshmen bring with them to campus. Some departments will provide a set of developmental composition courses (usually noncredit) after administering a placement test. The student is then required to satisfactorily complete that course before proceeding to the basic freshman level. There is usually less student anxiety, or chagrin, if a placement test is used to determine level of performance, rather than first permitting enrollment in the upper course and then moving down to the noncredit level later. The success of the student who must first enroll in the developmental level will also depend partially on how well the counselor interprets the test placement message. It will be facilitative to project a positive attitude about the developmental course so that the student will approach it with determination and a desire to succeed.

Integrative Career Information: Central to the counseling of black students for academic achievement is the inclusion of realistic career information. If the foundation information is not a part of the holistic advising process, then the student has a tendency to erroneously think of a referral to the Career Center as having no connection. Therefore, it is essential that the counselor integrate the information in order to give an impetus so that the student will take his or her own positive action with confidence. Visits to a well-established Career Center on campus should be encouraged, but the student should arrive there with some preparation from the counselor. It will make the referral clearer to the receiving counselor and, hopefully, beneficial to the searching student. Too often, understaffed campus units that specialize in the area of career information must spend most of their time setting up the necessary interviews for juniors and seniors to meet with prospective employers. This is too late for the freshmen to begin the journey on a successful academic program which may put them in line for a good job upon graduation. (See: **"Careers and Pathways."**)

MERITOCRACY

The wide use of tests in America emphasizing the need to judge personal attainment by performance is sometimes referred to as "meritocracy," a term first used by a British sociologist, Michael Young, in his book, The Rise of the Meritocracy (1958). He used the term to contrast it with "aristocracy," in which one ascends through the possession of money, power, and status via family and/or bloodline. In fact, the term fits the American educational scene quite well. All high school and college counselors are aware of the annual "Merit Scholars" who, because they have tested well, are granted fine tuition scholarships to the colleges of their choice. Some institutions of higher learning will brag about the large number of such students they have attracted each year. Right or wrong, high value is placed on the school system which ranks near the top nationally on standardized tests. It is an acceptable notion that such performance indicates good teaching is occurring.

Astin (1982) offers a thesis on standardized testing and the meritocracy which seems to infer ". . . that meritocratic practices can be contrary to the fundamental purposes of education and that continued reliance on meritocratic values in American higher education poses the single most serious obstacle to the educational progress of disadvantaged minorities." He further proposes that the discarding of meritocratic values will not only help minorities make progress but that all students will benefit from adherence to "purely educational values," which in time should substantially improve the quality of education.

TESTS AND SCORES

As a caution to this brief section on the highly controversial area of testing, counselors should be reminded of the awesome responsibility that accompanies the use of tests in education. Much good or harm can be done by the utilization of tests in the academic setting. The issue of testing is discussed here in the context of some of the effect on black students in higher education. There is no intention to make this discussion exhaustive or complete. This is not my area of expertise. (For further information on tests and testing procedures, see the **Bibliography**.)

Tests are so numerous that educators can easily get confused about which is the best for the purpose intended. Counselor training programs at the graduate level will usually require one or more courses in the skill of administering and interpreting tests and other measurements. Prospective counselors spend many hours practicing and learning the value of many instruments but frequently are limited to those in current, popular use. These are tests for predicting academic success. Even the test publishers disagree with their best "predictive supporters" and now place the company's emphasis on the tests' use as only one of several recommended measures for admissions purposes.

Perhaps there has been too much preoccupation with test scores and prediction for college achievement. Allport (1958) discovered that research on the increased use of the intelligence test indicated that "the more culture-free a test is, the smaller the group differences appear to be." No doubt Allport's statement helped open up the door on all tests so that in the subsequent years, many have been revised to reflect as much as possible that elusive "culture-free" quality.

It was proposed by Kenneth Clark more than two decades ago that the person who comes to the classroom with "the hidden curriculum" will achieve faster and better than that person who does not have such an advantage. For Clark, middle-class whites were the possessors of "the hidden curriculum" in the form of newspapers, magazines, books, pleasure travel, meaningful adult conversations and educational toys found in the home. The ghetto dweller, or economically disadvantaged child, would not have these advantages and would, therefore, remain behind in school unless some educational intervention took place.

Rankings are very important to Americans. Witness the value placed on the Nielson Ratings of the television shows and the lists of the "Fortune 500" businesses, the accredited colleges, top twenty athletic teams, political candidates, ad nauseum. American educators started early in the 20th century to use the intelligence and achievement tests to determine "excellence" and "quality." Perhaps the largest amount of group testing was first done in the military during

World Wars I and II when tests for literacy screening and educational competency for training purposes were administered to millions of recruits and draftees. The resulting perceived need for tests gave rise to a vast industry of testmakers and publishers in this country which continued through the middle Eighties.

TEST USE AND ABUSE

There is a long-standing debate over testing which centers on "construct validity." Can tests be "culture free" and yet test what they propose to test? The two largest test publishers and others who have researched the field usually defend their tests and the construction. Some of the critics of testing feel that the basic problem is not in the test itself but in the way it is used that creates problems for minorities. Any test, used as a device to screen-out, is a serious hurdle for blacks to leap over. But, conversely, when the test is used as a diagnostic tool in concert with other qualifying data, it becomes a special aid to the educator and a benefit to the student.

When the time finally arrived at my own campus (IUPUI) to institute a testing center, I was able to have some input on policy directions. The resultant policy stated that the testing program was for placement, not admission. It has done that job well in assessing student levels in English and mathematics, as well as in providing services for departmental advanced credit and other special tests as recommended by faculty and counselors for individual students. In this manner, the testing program does not harm minorities; rather, it assists them in their educational progress. This use of testing is positive and does not fall into the category of abuse.

PRE-COLLEGE ASSESSMENT

In response to a general national call for quality education, some academics have been urging the implementation of a new achievement test for high school seniors. This test is termed essential to help policy makers monitor the progress of education reform. "Reform," is fast becoming the "buzz" word in discussions focusing on public education in the U.S. Proponents of the new (yet not clearly defined) test state that colleges could use the device to supplement the other information which comes in on freshmen.

Measurement of student skills appears to be at the top of a lot of educators' agendas. Supporters of the concept are reported to be shaping up political support in Congress which would perhaps force the tests on all school districts that accept U.S. funds. Capitol Hill insiders seem to think that when the full plan gets to the lawmakers, there will be brisk debate on the issue.

It is not new or unusual to hear criticism of any plan that appears on the surface to be a short cut to excellence. Detractors from the national test plan include testing experts such as Educational Testing Service whose leadership said the proposal was flawed and misguided. Civil libertarians also believe that the test would fly in the face of a democratic, decentralized system of education. It would, in their view, dictate the use of the test for everyone.

A national test would of course, be very expensive. There are estimates that it would cost upwards of $90-million a year to administer -- something like $30 per test. The leaders of the plan who are concentrated in a group known as Educate America, would have the cost borne by the federal and state governments so that no student would face financial hardship. There will probably be long, heated discussions before this question is finally resolved.

PERSONAL ASSESSMENT INSTRUMENTS

By no means is the following list of assessment instruments intended to represent anything more than the author's own gleanings from the vast array of commercially available materials. My personal experience and that of my colleagues throughout the Indiana University System indicates that these are useful in many types of situations but should be used with considered discretion. Not any of them are panaceas, but each may individually be of help to black students as well as to his or her counselor in the search for direction. The instruments should be viewed only as an additional tool for making informed academic decisions. If you have a testing service on campus, or a Psychology Department interested in such assessment, consult with them on the use of these instruments and the resultant data. The test publishers will be pleased to send manuals and other pertinent information about their instruments so that you will be knowledgeable and use them correctly. Whenever possible, secure expert advice on tests and their administration so that students and the educational process will benefit.

Decision Making Inventory. Value assessment.

Differential Aptitude Test Battery (DAT). Aptitude for Management/Professional Occupations.

General Aptitude Test Battery (GATB). Aptitudes for all, but mainly for trades and skilled.

Holland Self-Directed-Search. Career/occupational satisfaction based on interests.

Myers Briggs Type Indicator. Learning style, information processing, occupation satisfaction.

Merkler Style Preference Inventory. Newly published instrument designed to help student make informed career choices. Uses RIASEC Codes. (Write to N. L. Merkler, c/o P.O. Box 2768, Indianapolis, IN 46206 for information.)

Self Descriptive Inventory.

Strong-Campbell Interest Inventory. Job satisfaction, environmental-value factors.

Word and Number Assessment Inventory.

RECENT RESEARCH FINDINGS

An important collection of research data, spanning more than ten years, was recently edited in a book by Professor Anne S. Pruitt (1987) of The Ohio State University education faculty. This compilation of previously published data summarized the various findings giving some attention to access for minorities to college and which factors most influenced their persistence. Although 21 educational and social recommendations were developed through a scientific analysis of the findings, certain ones for implementation by institutions of higher learning which could bring about improved black student enrollment and retention were:

Coping Skills Programs: These programs would teach students how to cope with the new demands they face in a college environment. Part of the program emphasis, as reported by the researchers, would include the cooperation of an alert faculty who would help identify, and even approach, students suspected of needing some adjustment in their personal coping skills. The next step in the process, it seems, would be to teach those skills through short, noncredit courses or workshops. Other opportunities for teaching include informal meetings in the dormitory lounges or other gathering places on campus where program staff can conveniently meet with students in the academic setting.

Ease of Transfer: The community colleges of the U.S. have had a continuing struggle with the universities in transferring their credits because of certain barriers. Those barriers should be removed and the students allowed to transfer at least elective credit for all college-level work done in the community college.

Black Faculty Needed: The predominantly white institutions need to increase their number of tenured black faculty members on campus to serve as role models and to provide inspiration for young students.

Professor Pruitt and her associates state in her book, In Pursuit of Equality in Higher Education, that the 1972 Adams vs. Richardson decision ordering the dismantling of dual systems of higher education had far-reaching impact. Interviewed for the July 1987 "Book Review" section of Black Issues in Higher Education, Dr. Pruitt concluded that the decision "challenged long-held beliefs about who should go where to college. It challenged stereotypic thinking about racial inferiority and traditional views of appropriate roles for men and women." Therefore, it would seem that a decision such as Adams would permit institutions with an affirmative action attitude to move with assurance and confidence in their attempts to improve black student enrollment and persistence in college.

BLACK STUDENT POST-SECONDARY ENROLLMENTS

Reviewing the data relating to minority representation among U.S. college freshmen, it was encouraging to see it rise by 50 to 100 percent from the mid-1960s to the mid-1970s. In 1966, only 5% of college freshmen were black students. The enrollments slowly rose to a high of 9.2% by 1980 (Astin, 1982). Despite such gains which led to an increased completion of baccalaureate degrees, later information as reported in The Chronicle of Higher Education and other educational journals indicates a leveling off to a decline. There is a great fear among those in leadership positions in the black community that a decline in college enrollments will signify a serious decrease of young blacks entering the recently opened range of professional careers.

Some of the factors affecting black educational progress beyond the high school are: early drop-out before graduation; low aptitude test scores; poor study habits; need for financial aid; low self-esteem; lack of encouragement to continue education; little or no career information; institutional barriers to admission; low high school grades; and nonacademic high school curriculum. Astin's studies of minorities during the Seventies seem to suggest that (and not surprisingly) when black students present themselves to college with high quality academic preparation, then the persistence factor is enhanced. Thus, the better prepared student has a better chance of completing the baccalaureate degree. No other single category of freshman or environmental variable appears to relate more frequently or more strongly to desired outcomes than pre-college preparation (Astin, 1982).

NINE

COUNSELOR BEHAVIOR
and CLIENT RELATIONSHIPS

COUNSELOR CHALLENGE AND RESPONSIBILITY

The academic counselor who is white has a special responsibility and challenge in dealing with the lives of black students. When the counselor's expectations and preconceptions prevent him or her from seeing the black student's true capabilities, there is a problem. Grier and Cobbs in Black Rage (1968) assert that students are responsive to the expectations of their environment, but they read clearly both the conscious and the unconscious messages sent by all around them. If the counselor persists in sending negative messages to his or her student, then the student tends to act on the basis of those messages and may perform at a comparably low level. If there are no realistic expectations not based on race or color, the student may feel there is no need to attempt to achieve.

At least for the last two decades, black students have expressed deep concern over the lack of genuine interest in them by white counselors or in their academic progress. As noted by Grier and Cobbs, there are certain factors supporting their claims which make academic achievement difficult for blacks -- prime among those factors are the discouraging teachers and counselors in an institutionalized opposition posture to a learned black community. The research of the noted authors illustrated that whites think it is proper for blacks to excel among blacks, but white school personnel experienced considerable anxiety if black students begin to academically "show up" whites.

COUNSELOR BEHAVIOR

One prescription for improving counselor behavior should begin with a genuineness which results from a better knowledge of his or her client's cultural and family background -- the social sciences of the group. The counselor must understand the goals, needs, and aspirations of his or her clients and act positively on such information. This does not mean prying irresponsibly or unreasonably into the client's personal life as a part of the process of advising for academic success. Counselors must be wary of looking at the color of the client's skin and trying to pull from a "bag of tricks" the right modality to use. The simple practice of empathy, knowledge of background, and the elimination of prejudice or unfounded fears by school personnel will put them in a good position for helping young black students to realize their dreams.

In a discussion of relationships, Vontress (1970) affirmed that "it is more arduous to establish empathy with those unlike themselves." There is, then, no facade or mask of sincerity, no persona that is equal to genuineness and honesty. Insincerity will be found out sooner or later -- mostly sooner -- by young black students who have an uncanny detection system for determining who is "real." They can simply observe such clues as word usage ("you people"), counselor body language (avoidance of touching the client -- even a simple handshake, or on the other hand, a touching in the form of rubbing the head of males and or patting a female in a sexually suggestive manner). One of the most hated signals of white racism is for a counselor to be so insensitive as to tell a racially-loaded story or joke and then to expect the black student to laugh at it. In a like manner, any counselor who talks down to or uses overly professional jargon with a client, sends a signal that he or she has limited educational expectations of that individual and so does a great disservice. Students who experience such insensitivity in the counseling setting will not return to that counselor for additional service, even if it means no academic advice at all. Additionally, the student will usually spread his or her unhappiness with the experience via the campus "grapevine," which may seriously limit the effectiveness of that counselor with the black student population.

In a like manner, Jones (1972) says that counseling is rendered difficult to impossible when one does not understand or appreciate and respect the subculture which the student represents. Thomas et al. (1972) observed that " . . . genuine respect for the black (person) means approaching him truly as an individual human being and without preconceived stereotypes. But the counselor must also consider his specific social experiences as with any other human being." Carl Rogers (1962) has said also that the relationship with the client is more important than test scores, records, and theories of achievement. He believes something good (for the client) can come out of their meeting.

THE HUMANISTIC COUNSELOR

In his discussion of the humanistic counselor, Harper (1975) listed four important conditions for effective counseling of black students on predominantly white campuses: "1. The counselor should possess and communicate humanistic qualities of maturity, mental health, and effective interpersonal relations. 2. The counselor should have a knowledge of the social sciences of black Americans. 3. The counselor should be familiar with techniques and theories that might be applicable in counseling blacks. 4. The counselor should understand the nature and the dynamics of the university and various means of effecting change within it." With these qualities firmly woven into their styles, white counselors will be able to serve their black clients effectively in a holistic manner.

It is equally important, too, that the person who counsels black students must have himself or herself "together" in order to project the mature person's concern for the client. This certainly involves being a warm, helpful, and perceptive person without succumbing to the impulse of psychologically getting inside another's head. An empathetic and understanding counselor must be free from prejudices and stereotypes about blacks, thereby increasing his or her effectiveness in the relationship. Carl Rogers (1958) poses one of several questions which he asks of himself before interviewing a client: "Can I let myself enter fully into the world of his (the client) feelings and personal meanings and see these as he does?" Moreover, Rogers goes on to query: "Can I enter it so sensitively that I can move about in it freely without trampling on meanings which are precious to him?" The lesson here is to practice empathy and provide clear, accurate information relating to the set of concerns that the student brings to the relationship. Too frequently, new counselors try to model themselves after a current "guru" in the field and unknowingly cut themselves off from the usefulness of the several other modalities which exist. Attempts by counselors to fit all clients into the framework of a single modality of treatment will generally lead their clients to perform at a low level of success.

STUDENT PROBLEMS

Both Gibbs (1973) and Vontress (1971) found that black students on white campuses generally have a set of problems which tends to slow or even arrest their academic development and progress. Related to the deterrents are: personal identity, expression of feelings to strangers, goals and objectives, academic expectations, and interpersonal relations. If a black student does not have a positive self-image, then he or she will suffer from a lack of positive aggression in the classroom, in the residence hall, or in other places on the campus where interaction is expected. Openness to others, however, is not a cultural trait of black

people. In fact, it may cause a student to withhold
vital information necessary to meet his or her own
needs. Not having been advised before arrival on campus
that setting goals is an important pre-college life
concern, the black student may find himself or herself
overwhelmed by what others might call normal academic
expectations and positive aggression.

The aware counselor puts to good use all his or her
knowledge about the client's background in a true
attempt to help move toward a recognizable goal
consistent with perceived needs, abilities, desires, and
strengths. With a solid understanding of the client and
his or her social sciences, the white counselor can make
a reasonable selection of techniques for use in the
counseling relationship. Alert counselors should be
aware that it is impossible to solve all the client's
problems in one session. In fact, white counselors who
expect that their personal charisma or campus reputation
will provide instant success in the relationship may be
facing disappointment. Trust is not easily given or
won. It must be earned, sometimes by paying a large
personal price. It may involve continued effort over a
period of time plus expression and actions of
genuineness on the part of the counselor who is often
considered by the student "to have all the answers."

MISLEADING MYTHS

As counselors strive to assist black students achieve
in school and build a sense of self-worth, they must be
conscious of the various myths that can be misleading.
Bayard Rustin (Ebony, 1979) defines these myths as "a
series of concepts that derive from wish-fulfillment or
a misperception of political reality." Whites, he
contends, because of their prejudices, fail to
differentiate among blacks. Thus, the attitude (or
thought) of "they are all alike" tends to influence
behavior of whites. Professionals are not excluded from
the large group of persons who act upon the basis of
myths, some of which have been passed down through the
generations as truth. According to Marie S. Bynum,
long-time school social worker, whites "do not recognize

that blacks have the same conflicts, differences of
class, and philosophy as any other American ethnic
group. "To deny this," she continues, "is in a sense to
perpetuate the illusion and to support the beliefs that
blacks are inherently different from whites, therefore,
not subject to the same laws governing human
behavior."(1970)

If the Black Studies programs of the Sixties and
Seventies have any lasting value, it is that they were
not premised on the existing American history books
which presented blacks only as a problem for the white
man. Black Studies should mean, even today, a
scholarly, objective inquiry into the place blacks have
held in the history of America. White counselors who
have the opportunity to partake of such courses or
programs will certainly benefit from such a rich
resource. It is an excellent method of learning the
social sciences of the black community and at the same
time, may serve to enhance the counselor's own academic
degree.

GOOD COMMUNICATION

If the white counselor is to be successful with black
clients, then he or she must be determined to
communicate. Black clients can be suspicious and
distrustful -- based on prior treatment of the client
and his or her family members by others in the wider
society. There is little history of black families
receiving "a fair deal" in prior relationships, whether
with a professional, sales clerk, legal authority or the
bus driver on the route.

Each individual client must be accepted by the
counselor as a person of worth, with a culture, values,
goals, and hopes for the future. Being nonjudgmental in
attitude, but firm and honest in presenting the facts,
is crucial to the academic advancement and ultimate
survival of the black client. As options are presented
by the counselor, the client must be permitted to make
his or her own decision. In many ways, this is a
teaching process .-- one the counselor needs to attend
with care, so that the client will understand and act

upon the information given in a mature manner. It also will serve to build a positive sélf-identity and to lead the client into the posture of trusting. As self-determination is fostered, the black client will exhibit changes in feelings and attitudes which can be readily observed. Helping the client to experience successes, no matter how small, will get him or her moving in a positive way toward academic achievement and all it implies.

In spite of the vast social distance already built into the relationship by the condition of race or color, it is possible for some black students to learn -- in time -- to trust a counselor who is white and, *ipso facto*, a member of the wider society which historically has not behaved responsibly toward black people. The counselor can help in relating by not being boxed in by the client's past or by his or her own. Perhaps, with empathetic understanding and being knowledgeable about the social sciences of the person across the desk, white counselors will be able to produce a more effective student/counselor relationship. While not easy to effect, remember that the client is **becoming** -- not already formed. In difficult situations, try to resist the opportunity to "set the student straight," but instead, use your own psychological maturity to foster client growth. It is the counselor's job to affirm the client, to accept his or her whole personality, and to set about developing the discovered potentials.

COUNSELING STRATEGIES

When viewing cases of student/counselor relationships, Stikes (1984) listed more than 20 useful strategies for developing good rapport. Among them are the following six areas which I believe to be most important and which should lead the list: 1) active counseling; 2) goal orientation; 3) assistance in seeking alternatives; 4) advocacy; 5) self-disclosure and genuineness; 6) recognition of feelings and behavior. While all of the Stikes strategies are helpful, the above six should assist a white counselor in focusing more clearly in the delivery of his or her professional services to black students. A brief but personal review of each of the six may be sufficient to renew the resolve of practicing professional counselors and to give them courage to continue.

Counselors need to be pro-active as they assist black students in their academic development by encouraging them to talk to classmates and to seek aid early in meeting the requirements of the course. It is well known that most students are reluctant to seek the professors because of a perceived fear of being rejected as a "dumb" or "lazy" person. One method of clearing the way for honest teacher inquiry is for the counselor to approach professors prior to the start of classes with a friendly question of: "If a student wishes to get a clarification on a course matter, should the student see you before, or after, the class meets?" The response you get will give clues as to whether the professor welcomes scholarly inquiry or rejects it out of hand as having no value. This should help you in counseling students who are having classroom problems. Care should be maintained so that students are not turned-off from certain professors who may not enthusiastically entertain the idea of being questioned outside the classroom. Remember, in most colleges it is expressly the professor's academic freedom to conduct the classroom in his or her own style. Sometimes there is a thin line to be observed by counselors and other personnel who should not interpose themselves as barriers between the student and the teacher. To do so is not only unprofessional, but undermines the collegial relationship which should exist on the campus.

As a counselor/teacher, it is necessary to help black students become aware of their own need to set realistic life goals and then to try to meet them. Many times you must clearly illustrate why goals are necessary and how they can assist in the student's personal development. If the counselor is truly aware of black social sciences, he or she will recognize that goal orientation may not be a solid part of living as a black in a white society. In fact, many black students will tell you that the setting of goals is generally considered useless since there is little or no control of one's life from the cradle to the grave. Your counselor role in this instance is to discover how to connect the goal with possible results for the student to believe. Your skill with and knowledge of interest inventories and other assessment materials will be helpful in determining career direction which is satisfying and realistic within the terms of the student's personal situation. (See: **"Tests and Scores."**)

As counselors meet with their black clients after classes have started, students want to and need to know clearly where they stand before the "mid-term brick wall" falls on them. You should teach through your counselor skills how to recognize possible failure early so they can be administratively withdrawn from the courses or take other alternative actions such as reducing work hours or getting tutor help. Finding acceptable alternatives for black students may very well be campus specific. Therefore, each counselor should personally investigate these alternatives to be assured that students are not thrown from one bad situation into another.

Being a student advocate requires much of the counselor. Paramount in that role are personal integrity, a willingness to take risks, and a good understanding of the campus rules pertaining to the situation at hand. It does not mean, on the other hand, that the counselor is to join the student body in a war of "us against them." It does mean, however, that the caring counselor may choose to advance himself or herself as a positive spokesperson who may disagree with the rules and, at the same time, endeavor to get them changed from within the university structure. Quite often, performing as an advocate on campus may unfortunately alienate some colleagues who mistake your proper role as "interfering," or "just being a busybody." Only you, the counselor, can determine if the circumstances you choose to enjoin are worth the risk involved.

When a counselor is able to lay bare his or her own values, fears, needs, or goals in the presence of others as a demonstration of honesty, then it may be possible for a black student to reciprocate and then begin to trust. Blacks want to be shown that a "genuine person" is seated in the chair on the other side of the desk. Just how much self-revelation is necessary for the student to understand you is relative to the situation and to your own personality. Only matters relating to the student's own circumstance are valid in the counseling interview, and all others are best left unsaid.

White counselors are often confronted by black students with statements similar to: "Professor Doe is prejudiced!" To respond with: "You don't mean that." is to deny that student's feelings -- whether they are real or imagined. That kind of counselor behavior discounts the student as not having enough sense to know when he or she has been discriminated against by some other person. The student behavior in such instances may range anywhere from stony silence to a vociferous outburst with the counselor as the target. At that point the counselor is perceived by the student as being prejudiced or, at least, uncaring. Recognition of feelings is important for the relationship to continue as a good one, even though you may not personally agree with the student's assessment of the situation. Counselors must continue with the student in a non-judgmental mode while listening to him or her through the anger or dismay as exhibited. It becomes your responsibility as the professional to help the student sort out the problem and arrive at some workable solution acceptable to the student. There will be days when such problems seem to usurp all of your time and energy. As a holistic, caring counselor who is student-centered, you should be able to meet the challenges and manage the situation well.

HOLISTIC COUNSELING APPROACH

When the counselor applies the holistic counseling approach to the student relationship, he or she helps the student to honestly cope with all the attending realities of life. All answers will not be suddenly apparent from the holistic posture, but the student should be able to work on acceptable solutions to the vast array of problems outside academics which may ultimately have profound effect upon the pursuit of higher education. It has been said many times before that "The whole child comes to school" -- that is so from kindergarten through college. Your client is concerned not only with the joys and struggles of getting an education but may also need to deal with being a part of a family, working a job, living in a dwelling, or maintaining relationships with family and friends. All of the above add daily stress and concern which can be debilitating or, at least, distracting to the student as he or she attempts to master the college classroom. It is the holistic-thinking counselor who is able to bring all the appropriate areas of concern into focus and onto the table for intensive scrutiny and work. (See: **"Holistic Process for Academic Counseling."**)

It is at this point of relating to the client that the counselor must also be a <u>teacher</u>. The student should be regarded as a pupil so that some of the behaviors needed to advance through the college system can be effectively taught. There should be no attempt on the part of the counselor to either by-pass or ignore the rules but rather to give an understanding of them and prepare the client for the necessary adjustments. Counselors also should teach personal goal-setting and use available diagnostic instruments to assess interest, learning styles and career direction. (See: **"Tests and Scores."**)

TEN

MANAGING YOUR OWN RACISM

RACISM'S TRUTHS

In his final, full-length book, <u>Where</u> <u>Do</u> <u>We</u> <u>Go</u> <u>From</u> <u>Here</u> (1967), the late Martin Luther King, Jr., said it was about time we heard the truth about racism in the U.S. and how it became so pervasive. It was his view that, "In human relations the truth is hard to come by, because most groups are deceived about themselves." It is principally a constant search for racial scapegoats and broad, baseless rationalizations for racist behaviors that bind people "to individual and collective sins." In a very spiritual mode, Dr. King also asserted that, "He who lives with untruth lives in spiritual slavery. Freedom is still the bonus we receive for knowing the truth." Quoting the Holy Bible he reminded the country that, "Ye shall know the truth, and the truth shall set you free."

The present dualistic society in the U.S. is the result of white America's split personality on the mammoth question of race relations. From the very beginning of this country when the Founding Fathers framed the Constitution declaring this a democracy, there was great ambivalence and even negativism toward black people because of their servitude status. There was, and still is, a love-hate attitude towards blacks which engulfs the country whenever the problem of racial

justice raises its head. It appears that white America
consistently has said that this is a land of freedom and
opportunity for all who meet certain standards of being,
but because of the conditions of birth, persons of color
cannot be fully included.
Social scientist Ruth Benedict in her Race: Science
and Politics (1947) likened racism to "the dogma that
one ethnic group is condemned by nature to hereditary
inferiority and another group is destined to hereditary
superiority." In essence, one group hopes that something
biological or physical will happen to eliminate other
"bothersome" races or, at least, make ethnically pure
the one holding superior status.

GENOCIDE IN HISTORY

History records many acts of genocide by one group
against another. The most ghastly and determined of
such acts was the attempt by Adolph Hitler to eliminate
the Jews, who were the Nazi Germany's scapegoats. The
Holocaust almost achieved the goal of the "Aryan
purists" who systematically killed more than six million
Jewish people throughout Europe because of their
ethnicity.
Today there are black Americans who feel strongly and
attempt to justify their claim that a form of genocide
has been practiced by white Americans toward people of
color. The thrust of the claim is that black Americans
are threatened with elimination through the racist
mechanisms of segregation, discrimination, economic, and
social deprivation. Counselors should be aware that
those feelings persist and are present in all black
psyches but perhaps potentially more openly volatile in
low socioeconomic class families in the black community.
Genuine concern and "attending to business" on the part
of counselors will help override some of these concerns
as you work with black youth in the academic setting.
It is a complex issue which is difficult for the black
student to explain or resolve alone. Respect for the
feelings of your clients, whether expressed or not, will
promote positive and clear communication, which is
essential in the counseling relationship.

CHANGING RACIST VIEWS

The wider American culture is built mostly on an illusion of stability and continuity. So if racist views are to be changed, then significant alterations also must come in the wider societal value system. Standards of societal behavior should no longer be based on an archaic European normative culture. There must be an allowance for the infusion of good and important culture traits as found in the Afro-American experience. These traits originate in the ancestral cultures found in most of Central and Sub-Saharan Africa. They are varied and contain many adaptable elements involving speech, music, crafts, language, social customs, art, religion, legends, and lore. White American society is the loser for not choosing to incorporate more of these traits and acknowledge their usefulness and value to the development of a nation and people.

It still may take generations for broad changes to be noted in the area of race relations in the U.S. In all probability, the changes will be gradual unless there is a major shift in the attitude of whites in power. It is likely that this kind of social change will occur only if it means no loss of control over the lives and fortunes of those now within the political and economic status quo. Despite slow social and economic advancement, there is hope in the black community that greater and swifter movement toward a truly equal society will develop along with an enlightened population. Therefore, it is important that excellence in education (and its delivery) truly become a part of this nation's public and private school systems as early as kindergarten and continue on through college.

EXAMINING YOUR OWN RACIAL ATTITUDES

The late Dr. Martin Luther King, Jr., once said in a speech: "The straitjackets of race prejudice and discrimination do not wear only Southern labels. The subtle, psychological technique of the North has approached in its ugliness and victimization of the Negro the outright terror and open brutality of the

South." (King, 1963) The condition that Dr. King described some years ago is now being experienced by black students throughout the country as they search for justice in the system. Currently, racist attitudes are considered by black youth as sub rosa and, thus, defy the gathering of sufficient evidence important enough to make a case for legal change. At this point in our history, it is also uncomfortable for whites to openly discriminate against any minority in the U.S. Public sentiment and present law will not support an individual or group wishing to stop the development or upward movement of black persons even though several recent attempts have been made by Neo-Nazi or Ku Klux Klan groups to publicly vent their racist views against those they hate.

In the book Staying O.K., Harris and Harris (1974) illustrated how the "Don't Messages" help to stymie individual lives and happiness because of the effect of negative injunctions. Black students, for example, are especially vulnerable to negative admonitions, having heard such all their lives: "don't show your feelings -- be cool; you can't get anywhere the white man doesn't want you to go; you don't belong here; don't take algebra -- it's too hard; don't go to college -- get a job." The aware counselor can help offset these negativisms by practicing a holistic approach to counseling and by recognizing the students' feelings. When a student learns that you not only "see" his or her feelings but that you accept the having of them without penalty, then a good relationship is begun. Being non-judgmental is a difficult attitude for any human to cultivate. It must then become a part of the counselor's persona if true and useful relationships are to be formed with students seeking academic assistance.

To help generate those "O.K." feelings, Harris and Harris (1974) suggested that eye contact and use of student names will reward you with trust. Listening, even while asking questions, will provide clues to the true, if not expressed, student need. To some degree, all students, regardless of ethnicity, will disguise the reason responsible for nonproductivity. Blacks will disguise their reasons even more. It then becomes necessary to "give yourself away" to the client to encourage the development of a solid relationship. If it is your style, perhaps the use of light humor may serve to loosen up your client in the interview. Humor used in this manner probably should have little or no connection with the reason why a student is seeking your aid. Caution is advised so that the honest smile or laugh is not mistaken for either a discounting of the client or a perceived distancing of the counselor. Being real in the eyes of the black student is very important for a continued and beneficial relationship.

AN INDICATOR OF PERSONAL RACISM

If a simplified and valid instrument existed which would identify clearly the root causes of prejudice and racism, most well-wishing people would opt for its use. Of course, there is no single device which will do this. Several years ago there was a very popular paper and pencil test which sought to measure one's knowledge about black people, their language, and cultural quirks. While it might have been fun to administer that particular test to white professionals who worked in black urban communities, it did not get at the underlying attitudes which foster racist feelings. After having stated that no perfect instrument exists to measure one's racism, I am tempted to pose here a few statements which suggest that all white people have varied levels of prejudice. These highly personal statements are presented not to shock, or to blame, but hopefully to stimulate the reader's thoughts and help identify possible areas of personal race relations or internalized feelings needing some change. The following check list is based on the "Social Distance Scale" first created by Professor Emory S. Bogardus (1959). He used the scale to measure the "degree of sympathetic understanding" that a group of surveyed people felt existed between themselves and other specified groups. His well researched and tested scale consisting of sixty statements centering on attitudes had a scoring system that gave a quantitative hierarchy. The following simplified check list (which I

have titled: "**Racial Distance Index**") has 25 items and
is designed **only to stimulate thought** and to focus the
reader's attention on his or her own racial feelings.
You are invited to determine your own "racial distance
index" on the form. Read the brief instructions and
then take the "**Index**" yourself.

RACIAL DISTANCE INDEX

The respondent should check those statements that most nearly approximate your feelings of social distance from black people. Do not analyze the statement -- just give **your first reaction toward blacks** based on your immediate feelings. Please check those statements which indicate the relationship you would be <u>willing</u> <u>to</u> <u>enter</u> <u>into</u> with blacks:

_____ to attend school together
_____ to join my fraternity, sorority, or social club
_____ to live in my apartment building or next door to my house
_____ to marry and live with as a mate
_____ to have my children attend the same school
_____ to stand in at my wedding
_____ to work beside me each day
_____ to be my pallbearer
_____ to date my teenage child
_____ to accept a blood transfusion
_____ to have as a boss
_____ to attend the same church
_____ to invite to my child's Baptism or Bar (Bas) Mitzvah
_____ to spend the night at my home as a guest
_____ to invite to sit at my table in a crowded restaurant
_____ to trust my health to a practicing professional
_____ to "baby-sit" my infant child
_____ to rent my house
_____ to give my infant child the same name
_____ to visit for personal or pastoral counseling
_____ to ask for a job reference
_____ to marry my adult child
_____ to share a telephone at work
_____ to invite to a family picnic
_____ to soak in the same hot tub

_____ **My Total Score**

To score: Count the number of check marks and <u>subtract</u> from the total of 25. The remainder should give you your "Distance Index." **A score of 13 or above indicates you probably have a considerable social distance from blacks.** You may need to consider some change of attitude or at least become aware of the racial prejudice content that the statement connotes in order to change future behavior. (See: **"Selected Reading List"** and **"Racism, Stereotypes, and Prejudice"** for valuable resources which may help an individual in making attitudinal changes.)

(Based on "Social Distance Scale" by E. S. Bogardus)

DYNAMICS OF PERSONAL RACISM

If you have scored yourself on the above "Index" and
discovered that personally a bit of racism is latent or
on the surface, then you owe it to yourself as a
professional to look for acceptable ways to make
positive change. Moreover, your black clients and
campus colleagues will also benefit from your personal
emotional, and social growth. Be assured that it will
show in time and that you will feel better about what
you know and what you do in the counselor-student
relationship. Martin Luther King, Jr., (King, C., 1983)
once said in a speech: "Like life, racial understanding
is not something that we find but something we must
create . . . it must be created by the fact of contact."
And that is what you as holistic counselors must do --
make positive contacts with the black students on your
campus to help them toward success.

Frequently, an argument used against making racist
changes sounds like: ". . . but I am only one person . .
." True as that may be, it is also the best plea for
getting the job done well. The desired, positive
response for change is: "Yes, I am one person, but as a
professional counselor I will endeavor to help one
person at a time." Permanent change requires continuous
intellectual honesty and the acknowledgement that you
have had significant negative attitudes and practices in
your life. You must then determine to open your
conscious mind and earnestly try to make a difference.
Anger, shame, or guilt should not become a residence for
the feelings you experience when a racist thought enters
your mind. The dynamics of personal change will help
you recognize and effectively resolve those feelings and
move your performance to its highest level. Your
challenge is to continually work at it with honest
commitment to achieve lasting results.

TEN SUGGESTIONS FOR CHANGING RACIST ATTITUDES AND BEHAVIOR

* Begin change by acknowledging that **you** are capable of harboring racist attitudes.

* Determine to learn more of the social sciences of the racial or ethnic group about which you have negative feelings. Search for readings which should help you change.

* Research your own social sciences to know yourself and your own racial group in greater depth. Self-knowledge can sometimes become a truly freeing experience.

* Refuse to repeat or pass along racist stories and attitudes expressed by others.

* Professionally operate from the stance of equality of personhood.

* Accept the psychological, sociological, and theological fact that there is no innately superior race or group.

* Realize that in the present society you need not be pathologic to indulge in acts of institutionalized racism. It becomes your task to escape the trap of following the crowd or assuming racism is justified because it has existed so long.

* Understand that racists are not mentally ill. The "sickness" of racism is not a medical diagnosis -- it is used as an excuse. All kinds of people are racists.

* Black people already know that racism is rampant in the U.S. This fact was finally admitted by the "Kerner Report" in 1968. Your attitudes towards black clients should undergo and sustain serious self-scrutiny for racist feelings.

* Believe that you can make a difference -- even though it may be only with one person at a time. As a professional counselor, you are in an ideal position to make change happen.

ELEVEN

CAREERS AND PATHWAYS

FUTURE WORK FOR BLACK AMERICANS

It is too simplistic and unrealistic for a counselor to think that all "well-prepared" young blacks will find appropriate work without something special being done to insure its happening. The career development pattern in the U.S. has not fostered such liberal and equal methodologies for achieving parity with white youth. In fact, there is ample historic evidence that deliberate negative behaviors have been, and are still being, used to limit the growth and upward movement of blacks on the career ladder in both business and government service. The specific need for affirmative action at various levels of employment is outstanding in the U.S. even in the waning 1980s. There seem to be no indicators to encourage the dismantling of the affirmative action process which is intended to insure that minorities are included in the hiring pool by the use of additional strategies to find and welcome those not ordinarily a part of the career group.

As the nation looks forward to the decade of the 90s and beyond, it will witness some significant changes in the employment pattern and its character. Most of the projections being made concerning the future employment picture suggest that the new technologies will create some new jobs and that others will disappear. Some industries will grow faster than others while new ones will emerge, principally through the hard work of entrepreneurs who find and fill a community need. Most changes will be affected by the changing economy, health care of the population, social and political factors, the environment, and the interdependence of all these named, and other factors.

POPULATION AGE GROWTH

It is well known that the upper age level of the U.S. population has increased markedly with each decade since the 1960s. Census reports and insurance actuaries all predict that the number of persons over 65 years of age will grow to a staggering high. There are presently more than 100 persons 100 years of age and older in the state of Indiana according to the Social Security Administration which distributes pension checks to the elderly each month. The number may increase with the improved health care and nutrition advances the elders enjoy. It is expected that a similar occurrence will also be found in other states.

The teenage group is declining in the late 1980s to the extent that "fast-food" restaurants are finding it difficult to staff their stores with high school students who work for less than the minimum wage. As a result, managers are forced to advertise for full-time workers and offer liberal fringe benefits. Some employers are asking that retired (and able) persons return to the work force now that studies and experience have shown that older workers are more reliable and patient and bring stability to the workplace. In addition, the elders are eager to be useful again and willingly work at their tasks without constantly being directed by a supervisor. The arrangement works out fine for both the worker and the employer.

More former homemakers are entering the workplace, frequently without specific training for a particular job. They are quite content to begin working part-time while the children are still in school. Their work supplements the family income and gets the mother and wife out of the house for a part of the day where she interacts with other people on the job. It is good for her own mental health and permits her to ward off stagnation brought on by boredom in the house while everyone is out each weekday. The current high U.S. divorce rate also has driven the mother-homemaker out into the job market in order to support dependent children who are frequently awarded to her by the court. Too often the fathers of these children are expected and ordered by the court to pay support for their children, but that goal is seldom met in its entirety. Therefore, the children suffer if the mother is not employed and must depend upon the state welfare system to care for her family.

Black women have been noticeably absent from the Women's Movement despite efforts of white feminists to insinuate that the struggle of white women is synonymous with that of black women. On the contrary, black women have always been "liberated" and had to work out of necessity in the hope that they could contribute sufficiently to the family's meager income and rise above poverty. Since the freeing of the slaves, many black women have made homes for their own families and have worked in white homes as domestics, often leaving their own children alone or with a relative or older child in order to care for the offspring of their employers. Many times this unusual "devotion to duty" has gone unnoticed and unrewarded in terms of being paid a decent living wage for the job done. The counselor should be cognizant of such pressing family conditions and all the ramifications which may, in turn, affect black students' academic and social progress. That is not to say that all black students' families are fashioned in this manner, but it is likely that most white counselors will meet with students whose parents have both worked at low-level, low-paying jobs all of their lives. Such is the unhappy fact of life for the majority of blacks who constitute the lower socio-economic rank of the community. (See: "A Look at the Modern Black American Family.")

EQUAL OPPORTUNITY IN EMPLOYMENT

The Civil Rights Movement in the U.S. contributed greatly to the formation of federal policies which expanded equal employment opportunities for many blacks in the Seventies and Eighties. The growth of the black middle class included those young persons who reached that status through improved access to higher education, better business opportunities, and affirmative action. If it had not been for all these positive variables, many young blacks would never have ascended the socioeconomic stairs to thereby reach a reasonable "landing" for themselves and their families.

When asked by interviewing counselors (including at my own campus) why they wanted to attend college, the most frequent answer black students give is: "I want a good education so I can get a good job." Their emphasis is placed primarily on preparation and the need for better economic conditions within the black community. The implication is that the "green power" of money has an almost magical effect in breaking the cycle of poverty especially found in urban settings. With increased income, the black family is able to purchase better housing and health care which will go far in improving their living standards and, consequently, provide an avenue for enriched lives. Counselors need to be reminded that the majority of black students will arrive on campus from the urban community carrying all the heavy baggage of those who have not been a part of the social and economic middle class. While some general assumptions might be made concerning these students and their experiences in their own neighborhoods, it is important that each one be dealt with as an individual in his or her own right. Some whites may find it easier to generalize and thereby fall into the bad habit of stereotyping or placing students into a special box which has a nailed-down lid. Counselors who care should resist such behavior while realizing that the career and economic needs and social goals of Black Americans are very important in their search to achieve a part of the "American Dream."

104

CHANGES IN EMPLOYMENT IN THE FUTURE

If one chooses to review the economic predictions and forecasts of the Eighties, it is important to get at least an overview of the factors which set the trends and to take a look at the prospective level of U.S. employment in the Nineties. Some factors listed in the Occupational Outlook Handbook (1984-85) include: 1) consumer desire for improved and new products; 2) government regulation for consumer protection; 3) expansion or decline in "the smokestack industries"; 4) technological change, e.g., the introduction of more automated manufacturing equipment; 5) changes in the manner in which goods are produced and services rendered; and 6) other factors relating to overall U.S. Government fiscal and monetary policies, imports, and exports.

There are those in the black community leadership on national and local levels who predict in speeches and in reports such as the Urban League's Annual Report (1986) that all of the above changes in employment will mean less for blacks and other minorities. Many charges have been leveled which state that underemployment and unemployment will rise dramatically unless there is some positive intervention. Anything less than the application of massive remedies, the black leadership asserts, means the development of a "permanent underclass." (Gordon, 1965)

HIGHER EDUCATION AS A PATHWAY

While many career opportunities may actually begin to lessen in total numbers, counselors need to continue to urge black students to enter a wide range of preparation through higher education. Not only should there be movement toward the biological sciences, teaching, engineering and technology, medicine, nursing, and the legal profession, but the liberal arts another fresh look as an area for excellent development. As an example, many prospective employers in the vast service-oriented field now prefer that their new employees be "people people" in an effort to humanize their offerings. Development of career information resources that speak directly to the needs, salary, working conditions, outlook for the future, and specific preparation is necessary so that the counselor may correctly inform his or her students. Black-oriented publications such as Ebony, Essence, Black Enterprise, and Black Collegian should be a part of the counselor's personal library to learn of the current social sciences and some of the more important goals of black students and their families. If your campus or community library does not subscribe to such publications as listed above, then request that they be put on the acquisition list the next time the library's operational budget is prepared. These suggested magazines are only a part of a larger list which can be supplied by the nearest library's information desk.

As you help students in making informed academic major choices, remember that their goals and horizons can be lifted if careful planning and solid academic work is done. You, as the counselor, can become the catalyst which blends the information, student ability, goals, and other factors so as to arrive at a realistic career decision. It will not be easy. It shall require a lot of hard, earnest, caring work on the part of the counselor in tandem with the student's effort in the classroom. The ultimate proof of the job well done is clearly exhibited when your students persist to graduation and placement in jobs that match the education and skills he or she possesses. Perhaps then you will experience the greatest payoff of this giving profession by the elated feeling of joy when your students succeed.

Higher education is still considered by the black community to be a desirable path to the sharing of the American "good life." It is a goal hard sought by families in which there are no college graduates or persons who even attended any post-high school academic institution. Unfortunately, many of the opportunities for attending college are based on the ability to pay. Hard economic times have pressed the majority of black

106

families into such low-paying jobs or into chronic
unemployment to the extent that the higher education
dream grows dimmer. Budgetary choices made by the
federal government in recent years have greatly reduced
the availability of financial aid to the economically
disadvantaged of this nation. This fact necessarily
means fewer black high school graduates are able to plan
for college which they need for future employment in a
rewarding career. Counselors need to be encouraging and
resourceful so that black clients will continue and new
ones will apply for college admission in the future.
The black community, as well as the wider community,
needs to be assured of a continuing flow of prepared
professionals and other liberally trained persons to
work and lead in the days to come.

CAREER INFORMATION SOURCES

    If you do not have an active "Career Information
Office" on your campus, then it is extremely important
that you develop a list of sources where students can
get the assistance they need to make good
academic/career choices. To this end, you may wish to
fill a bookcase shelf or a file drawer with materials
you have gathered by writing to trade associations,
professional societies, business firms, and other
educational institutions. Try to place these materials
where students can see and use them conveniently --
while waiting for an appointment, on assignment, or just
browsing for ideas. To depend entirely upon the campus
office of "Career Information" may not be possible
unless you have a clear and cooperative relationship
with that office in reference to your making student
referrals. At any rate, you should make available to
your students some of the basic printed materials from
which you can suggest that the student read and even
copy pertinent information. Many free or low-cost
career materials are available if you write and ask for
them. You should also be able to add your own local
sources to the following suggested list:

CAREER INFORMATION
SOURCE LIST

* The Occupational Outlook Handbook. Washington D.C.:
  U.S. Dept. of Labor. Bulletin 2205, 1984-85.

* Employment Security Agency (State).

* College library.

* Film Strips, cassettes, tapes, and kits of
  occupational information prepared by commercial
  firms.

* The Black Collegian. National Magazine of Black
  College Students. New Orleans: (Quarterly).

* Computerized information systems.

* Job service offices of the U.S. Employment
  Service.

* Local personal contacts with persons successfully
  practicing in the career.

* Financial Aid Information Office on campus.

* City or County Employment Service Office.

* Local public library.

* Local or regional industry and business personnel
  departments.

* Local and state government employment offices.

* Classified sections of local newspapers and
  magazines.

While there must be close interaction between the student and the counselor who is advising on career choice, the ultimate decision belongs to the student. The counselor must put at the student's hand all the support that can be gathered from inside and outside sources. Among the human resources you can choose from are alumni, peers, retired persons who succeeded in a career, faculty, and workers in the local community. It is essential that career and life-planning be well integrated with academic advising for best results. Counselors need to keep their occupational information and skills up-to-date as economic conditions change swiftly in the U.S. Reading and attending workshops and conferences involving career decision making should help provide the continuing education needed to help students make good choices.

EMPLOYERS LOOK FOR THE "RIGHT STUFF"

Counselors can help the black college student prepare to show the "right stuff" to a prospective employer when faced with the big interview. No student should go unprepared to visit with a representative of a hiring firm. The student must appear and participate in the interview with confidence and other positive attributes in order to convince the "rep" that he or she should have that job. With a bit of research the counselor can determine some of the student characteristics which are being sought. This knowledge, along with specific tips gleaned from the large selection of current books on resumes, job interviewing, dressing for success, communication skill development, and similar information, should give you insights for helping your black clients succeed. Of course, the student needs to begin with a respectable G.P.A. and develop a right combination of characteristics to make up an attractive package of the "right stuff." Ultimately, personnel representatives will be looking for good attitudes, motivation, and that most elusive quality known as potential.

When a student presents himself or herself at your office with questions and worries about the future and jobs, the counselor should be prepared to offer basic information and a good referral. Unless your job description calls for full service in career information, you should not try to specialize in the field. There are several computer-assisted systems for presenting career material. You should investigate them in terms of whether or not the material speaks to the needs of your black clients. Several of the software programs on the market are both lengthy and expensive, but a library search will uncover some of shorter duration and lower cost. If properly used, electronic assistance can expand the knowledge and time of the counselor as you seek to move students through the educational pathway to success.

When one looks at the employment market during the final years of the Eighties, it is significant to note that a lot of energy and effort must be put into finding a good position. Counselors can be of great help to black clients who are in the job market by helping them conquer their natural fears of an interview and teaching them how to cope with the accompanying stress. Your own personal experience in job interviewing should be of value as you assist the student in preparation for an important meeting with a stranger who is looking for a worker. If there is a primary key for the interviewing process it. is <u>communication</u>. Much of the interview will, of course, center on how well the interviewee presents himself or herself by way of the voice. Personal appearance helps, but the ability to verbalize clearly about one's experience, training, desires, goals, and other personal data will often make the difference between one client and another. Students should be urged to prepare well for the job search and perhaps be given an opportunity to practice interview skills on the counselor who can then critique for effectiveness. (You may want to photocopy **"Some Tips For Surviving The Job Interview"** for your student.)

SOME TIPS FOR SURVIVING THE JOB INTERVIEW

(Most job placement experts suggest some variation of the following list of strategies for successful interviewing with a personnel representative. With your student select those items he or she needs most to work on. This list may be photocopied for your student.)

+ Be punctual. Arrive on time for the interview.

+ Dress appropriately. "Dress for Success!" Look like an employable person.

+ Smile and be friendly. Establish rapport with the interviewer as soon as possible. Don't be afraid to extend your hand in greeting. Make it a firm shake.

+ Relax. Use relaxation techniques such as meditation, deep breaths, or whatever calms your nerves--but no medication -- unless prescribed specifically by your physician.

+ Listen carefully. Be observant, but listen to the interviewer's questions and answer in clear "Standard English."

+ Ask questions. Later on in the interview, or toward its end, ask the questions you have previously planned.

+ Sell your skills. Communicate well with your voice, avoiding slang and off-color verbiage.

+ Be interested in the job. Know something about the company and the position you have applied for, and show enthusiasm.

+ Sit comfortably. Wait until offered a chair, then sit in a relaxed position but not sprawling over the furniture.

+ <u>Practice</u> <u>honesty</u>. If you don't know the answer to a question, don't try to fake it. Remember, the interviewer knows a lot more about the position and the work than you do.

+ <u>Do</u> <u>not</u> <u>smoke</u>. Chewing gum is also frowned upon.

+ <u>Take</u> <u>notes</u>. Use a small note pad and your own pen to write down those details (e.g., salary, location, interviewer's name, etc.) you might forget. You may take along a small briefcase or folder for extra copies of your resume and any other needed papers.

+ <u>Close</u> <u>the</u> <u>interview</u> with a cordial "Thank you!" for the time and opportunity to speak for yourself as the best applicant for the position. Ask the interviewer how <u>you</u> fit into their plans for the future and when you should look forward to hearing from them. Finally, tell the interviewer how interested and enthusiastic you are about that particular position.

+ <u>After</u> <u>the</u> <u>interview</u>: Evaluate your own performance in the interview. Did you follow the "Tips for Survival"? Send the interviewer a handwritten note of appreciation on plain stationery, thanking him or her and the company for the time spent with you. Did you think it was a success? What would you do differently in another interview? Make plans for the next interview with the same care and energy. Jobs are hard to get today and the competition is tough, but **YOU** can do it!

(Source: <u>Black</u> <u>Collegian</u>)

TWELVE

UPDATING THE DECADE OF THE EIGHTIES

THE STATE OF THE BLACK AMERICAN COMMUNITY

Black Americans believed that the decade of the Eighties would become the leavening period in the search for equal opportunity in the land of their birth. Unfortunately, that was not to be. Not only did the economy decline, but the level of racial understanding stepped off the edge of decency and hope. The projected growth of a larger black middle class did not happen. Instead, the earlier gains were soon to be overshadowed by a burgeoning new "underclass" that in the early Nineties is overwhelmed and characterized by single-parent households, poverty, ill health, crime, drug abuse, illiteracy, and homelessness.

Black America is frustrated, angry, confused, and in serious danger of sliding down the road of social, economic, and political disaster. Their view of a "kinder and gentler nation" is so dim that it dampens any thought of gaining equity with White America.

The following pages will comment on much of the above and other events that will ultimately have a profound effect on the future of the American black community. The overview of the Eighties (and peering into the Nineties) is provided to illustrate how much farther the nation must go on its journey toward equal justice and equal opportunity for all its citizens.

BLACK FAMILY DIVERSITY

In recent writings, Billingsley (1990) hoped that the general public in America understands that the negative concepts by which Black Americans are known do not represent the total picture. While three pervasive concepts (poverty, children in trouble, and single-parent homes) gather our attention, they foster an unfortunate set of false impressions. In one instance, the unwary might perceive of all of the single-parent families as inherently dysfunctional. Second, it becomes easy to generalize that those families not falling within the guidelines of these major concepts have no concerns or problems that require attention. Nothing could be farther from the truth -- in both instances. A danger still lies in the narrow study of families by well-meaning social scientists which brings forth false theories of black family life. That could lead to inappropriate remedies for ills within the black family. The full range of problems of the black family needs to be studied for full understanding before proposals for solution are implemented.

There is great concern being expressed about the current "marriageability" of the African American male and the growing number of mateless adult black females. It is feared that with fewer men to choose from, black women will suffer socially and economically and perhaps find themselves outside the domains of wife and motherhood. This serious condition began with the extensive loss of black male life in the thirteen-year war in Vietnam. It gathered momentum with the destructive forces of substance abuse, enormous unemployment, and crime in our cities. Various researchers have projected that a sizable portion of black males of marriage age will either be incarcerated or dead from street crime by the turn of the century. That is a frightening and serious statistic -- sure to be felt within the black community as it struggles to reach parity with the established white community. These facts threaten the well-being of the black family and offer little hope for the future.

Following the "American Way" of doing things, black
Americans still hope that their college-age daughters
will find a "good husband" while in school. Few of the
young black women date and marry white males. On the
other hand, more black male college students date white
females and eventually marry them. Studies have been
done on predominantly white college campuses which
indicate that, in many instances, the scarcity of black
women in the student body gives black men fewer choices
for dates. Anecdotally, young white women seem to be
attracted to the "dark and forbidden" in spite of their
being socially programmed by the white male standard
setter. Many of these relationships have a difficult
time on campus, but they persist. The campus social
climate can help or hinder their progress by its own
character. Under the rules of American freedom, cross-
racial associations should present no problems, but
current racism revival on college campuses destroys that
Constitutional right for some people. The campus
administration and student leadership need to press for
the end of racial enmity whenever it occurs.

Many years ago, W. E. B. DuBois (1971) pleaded for
the majority community to see blacks from a broader
point of view, not just as a simple problem. That
appeal is still critical today in order for stereotyping
not to occur from concentrating on a single social issue
such as poverty. There needs to be a more "holistic"
point of view from which all facets of the black family
can be appreciated.

Although the marriage relation is central in the
black family, it has declined as it has in the dominant
society. Black persons who marry, then divorce, usually
try to marry once more, sometimes to the same ex-spouse.

A recent (1989) conference at UCLA attempted to study
the marriage relation in the black community. It is
perhaps too early for reports to indicate reliable
trends in commitment to marriage by black men and women.
Various aspects of the future of the black family may be
in jeopardy, but the sense of family is so strong among
blacks that an estimated seventy-five percent live in a
family household. With a redefinition of the

traditional family setting, the following list of
alternative structures may contain the salvation of the
black family as an institution (Billingsley in State of
Black America, 1990):

1. Single-Person Households
2. Cohabitation
3. Children, No Marriage
4. Marriage, No Children
5. Marriage and Children
6. Children and Relatives
7. Blended Families
8. Dual-Earner Families
9. Commuter-Couple Family

As stated elsewhere in this book, African American
people are a diverse group affected by social class the
same as white America. In favoring the holistic view of
blacks, one can observe the differences in class and not
be reduced to stereotyping and reliance on myths. The
sociological concept of class maintains that a family
with greater economic, political, educational and social
resources and/or attainment has greater control over the
lives of its members than a family found in the
"underclass." Given that as a general measure, black
people find themselves fitting into a set of social
classes which range from upper to lower, depending on
the number of criteria used to make the judgment. The
number of class groupings may also be defined in a
variety of ways, depending on the social scientist
making up the list. Five social classes are currently
ascribed to American black societal structure: upper,
middle, working class (nonpoor), working class (poor),
underclass (nonworking poor) -- (U.S. Census). These
categories seem to work well in describing the economic
status of members of the black community.

Most of the black students being recruited for
predominantly white campuses are a part of the working
class (nonpoor), Many will be the first generation of
their families to seek higher education. The rest of
the black enrollment will mostly come from the two

higher classes with a minuscule amount arriving from the underclass. These factors need attention from campus authorities (including counselors) in a holistic manner so that academic achievement may become the rule and not the exception.

YOUTH UNEMPLOYMENT IMPACTS COLLEGE PLANS

An overview of racial equality in economics during the Eighties reveals no improvement from the previous decade. All quantifying indicators used by sources such as the U.S. Department of Commerce, Bureau of the Census, and Department of Labor, demonstrate a widening gap between blacks and whites in per capita income. It is still a fact that whites receive more money for comparable work than blacks. Equally true is the need for a black family to have two full-time incomes (husband and wife) in order to achieve the purchase of a home and the niceties of middle-class life.

The importance of these economic facts of decline in per capita income for black families suggests that fewer will be able to afford any education beyond public high school for their children. Such a drop in family income throughout the black community indicates that many more persons will descend into the working poor or into the underclass. Descent into the latter means that the wider community is faced with support of more indigent people who see no way up. They become doomed to a generational, marginal, dependent existence.

The American economy made many technological changes over the decade of the Eighties resulting in fewer entry-level jobs for youth to choose from. Most of the jobs that recent U.S. Government Administrations felt they created were low-paying positions within the fast-food industry. Thus, as youth graduated from high school, there was little in the way of employment to help with post-secondary education. The low-waged jobs could not support them if they had to be on their own. This hard economic fact prompted many black youth to enter the Armed Forces as an alternative to gainful employment. There, both male and female have found that

upward mobility is possible. It remains to be seen
whether the armed forces experience will help these
youth to enter the civilian community work force at a
later time.
When a black youth's parents become unemployed, the
family is profoundly disadvantaged. They are, by
previous conditions, less likely to have reserve
financial resources to call upon. Racial disparities in
income are large and thus the intensity of the problem
deepens. The lack of good employment in the black
youth's family discourages him or her in the search for
academic achievement. It is extremely difficult for
people in poverty (or in the underclass) to have lofty
aspirations. Finding the source of daily survival
becomes the driving force within the family unit.
Throughout the Eighties many large industrial plants
and factories either closed, reduced their staffs or in
the worst case, sent the jobs overseas. Industry issued
various reasons for such actions, including automation,
reduced inventory and union problems, but the
outstanding unspoken reason was the bottom line. In a
business atmosphere where takeovers and mergers were
rampant, the American worker was lost. Black youth
became the largest single group of unemployed and
underemployed in the nation. All the publicity about
the economy sent a signal to black youth that life after
school was too hard, so it is probably not worth the
time to try harder. If given no hope, most youth cannot
persist on their own. If they are truly "the men and
women and leaders of tomorrow," then they deserve the
full support of government, business, and industry.
As we advance into the Nineties, there seem to be no
definitive plans being made to give relief to youth who
seek employment during or after high school. That
critical topic has to become one of the agenda items on
the list of public policy priorities. Legislation at
the city, state, and national levels needs to be
developed posthaste. If not, the adage "Pay a little
now, or pay a lot later" may unfortunately become the
rule.
Knowledge of the general economy is something that
most college administrators and trustees discuss with

118

regularity. The seriousness of the problem and how it
affects college-age students and their families can be
addressed in part by on-campus employment opportunities.
There are many types of work that students can perform
if given the chance and a decent wage. Most colleges
subscribe to equal opportunity in study and work. They
can certainly help alleviate the financial problems for
some of their students by the development of a work
program. If such a program does not exist on your
campus, then, as change agents, counselors can serve as
a catalyst in its development. What can you do? First
start a discussion of the need with the campus movers
and shakers. Things should move forward from there.
Use your expertise and that of others in the community
who deal with careers and work to convince the
administration that the project is worthy and deserves
not only attention, but funding as well.

THE RISING FINANCIAL AID BATTLE

As the Eighties moved along, the available funds for
student financial aid drastically decreased. The need,
on the other hand, increased dramatically. It became
increasingly evident that, in order to develop diverse
campus enrollments, more financial aid and less loans
were needed to help minority college youth. Black youth
families in particular were in the unenviable position
of being so low on the economic ladder that large
educational loans were accepted. Some of these loans
will hang like a cloud over their heads for many years
to come, making it difficult to make economic progress
after graduation.
Throughout the decade, colleges and other post-
secondary institutions designated minority scholarships
in order to recruit and retain students of different
racial and cultural backgrounds. The process worked.
The educational institutions considered such awards
necessary and common in occurrence. In fact, financial
aid officers at many colleges recall that scholarships
have been widely praised by educators. The general
experience over the last thirty years of the concept of
designated minority scholarships has been a sound method

for attracting students to colleges. Many deserving black students received such aid which helped them to make economic progress toward a degree. At the end of the year 1990, a newly hired assistant secretary in the U.S. Department of Education made a startling ruling that it was illegal for a college to offer a scholarship only to minority students. This had a stunning effect on college administrations. The unsolicited ruling was probably generated by the controversy raised over reports that college officials planned to take receipts from the Fiesta Bowl collegiate football game and create minority scholarships.

Needless to say, a fire storm of protest burst upon the Department of Education resulting in somewhat of a reversal of policy. Liberal proponents of campus diversity campaigned and lobbied hard for the rule to be totally rescinded, but the White House only promised to review the policy. There were conservative groups that praised the ruling, probably giving courage to those who would revive blatant racism in education. At year's end, the ruling was generally considered faulty in legal reasoning and was called "a mean streak" by civil-rights activists. It is hoped that the "review" will be favorable toward the minority students who depend on such awards in order to attend college.

COUNSELOR EDUCATION NEEDS FOR DIVERSE STUDENT BODY

In many regions of the nation, educational entities are busy discussing the need to change the teacher and counselor education curricula. The entrance of more minorities and older students into the halls of academe demands a revision for counselor training programs. The graduate schools need to consider certain reforms in order to produce the type of counselors who can relate well to the "new majority" on campus. A changed curriculum should include at least the following suggested additions:

1. A requirement for all counselors in training must include quality courses in black history, urban education, culture in the black community, multicultural

program development, social sciences of the black community, and race and ethnic relations.

2. Counseling textbooks need to be updated to include minorities as opportunities rather than problems. They should emphasize the value in the differentness found in a racially diverse population.

3. Assignment of white counselors in training to practicums within educational centers found in the black community.

4. Schools of Education should hire black professors with the aim of providing a racially diverse faculty that will relate effectively to white students.

5. Schools of Education should help white counselors learn how to manage their own levels of racism so that black students feel a degree of comfort in the relationship.

ROLE MODELS AND SELF-ESTEEM

Each time I read an article on "role modeling" that focuses on famous persons and the <u>one</u> person who was instrumental in their early development, I am urged to list my own set. If it had not been for my parents who gave me the first models to follow, I certainly would have developed differently. My mother taught me formally, and, by example, how to relate to persons of the other sex. My father, on the other hand, demonstrated the value of the hard work ethic. Together they helped me to manage the legal racial discrimination and segregation we lived under. Without their combined interest in my wellbeing, I probably could not have achieved in any sense. For their loving care and direction, I am indeed grateful.

My other role models were many and emerged in various phases of my life. I remember Miss O. A. Smith, my fifth-grade English teacher, who drove home the basics of grammar; my Aunt Orel, whose infectious laughter and storytelling ability I still wish to emulate; Mr.

Bennett, who tried his best to teach me the higher levels of mathematics; Dr. Benjamin Quarles, history professor, whose writing and teaching styles I have tried to copy; Miss Myrtle Banks, high school teacher extraordinaire; Dr. Joe Taylor, mentor and friend (of nearly forty years); Mr. E. Belfield Spriggins, art teacher and a human rights inspiration; and many others who either spent time with me or whom I observed from afar. They all shared information and offered encouragement which I think made the difference.

As a counselor, you can provide a useful model for students to see by simply having your own life and "stuff" together. One does not have to be a famous entertainer or an outstanding athlete for others to emulate. Sure they are successful and, if it is possible, arrange to have your black students meet with these people who can inspire. Sometimes though, a local black community leader, teacher, minister, housewife, career woman, or other worker may be the one who can help youth see themselves in a more positive light. You should find ways to reach out into the black community and search for those people who have achieved and are willing to spend a little time with your students. One-on-one relationships are by all means the best, but exposure to a group of students will also help young people to find worth in themselves.

Much has been said about the need for individual self-esteem if people are to succeed. Psychologists and sociologists tend to agree that there are no easy "ten steps" to finding self-esteem. The route is much longer, circuitous, and often uphill. Black Americans are not very comfortable in taking personal problems to a psychologist. In all probability, the professional is white and necessarily requires that the client "tell all." Persons from dysfunctional homes tend to have low self-esteem. Sometimes when black people are faced with overwhelming problems they feel that there is no place to go. Many will resort to the use of drugs, alcohol, sex, gambling, overeating, or some other debilitating activity. The hope is to find relief from the painful problems. Oftentimes the remedy becomes worse than the affliction.

If one looks at the portrayals of blacks in Hollywood, or on television, the image presented for generations is one as a personal servant, a criminal,or a fawning entertainer. Such depictions are not positive and give youth nothing to help develop good self-esteem. The aware counselor will be careful about his or her use of certain entertaining figures as examples for black clients to look up to. Self-esteem, so say the psychologists, is at the root of our lives. Feeling good about ourselves is important to a healthy and happy life. Black students must have help in finding the formula of self-worth. Counselors should prepare themselves to offer that assistance whenever the need arises.

As more families become female-headed, it becomes vital to help the children and young adults learn how to become the best of adults. Counselors can assess the individual needs as they relate to students in an office session. Working together over a period of time will help that student to achieve personally and academically in college. Time, energy, caring, professional assurance, and knowledge are all needed to make the educational system work for black students. Few of today's black students have enough self-esteem. Caring counselors have an excellent opportunity to help them find it.

THE RISE OF RACIAL INCIDENTS ON CAMPUSES

The national media and the educational journals have been reporting on the racial problems found on college campuses during the mid-Eighties and on into the last decade of the century. These incidents seem to arise chiefly on predominantly white campuses. There appears to be no geographical area of the country that is exempt. They range from slight affronts to deep hatreds expressed by burning crosses, epithets written on building walls, negative characterizations of blacks on flyers and in fraternity party themes, and other public situations.

Early on, college administrators tended to believe that "boys will be boys" until the intensity rose and resident blacks (and whites) protested the lack of corrective action. Some Presidents and Deans immediately called for censure and ordered the campus security (or called the local police) to investigate for prosecution purposes. Whenever swift action was taken, the incidents seldom recurred. But where there was no, or slow, action, other incidents happened. Apparently, the perpetrators felt emboldened if no one spoke out against the racist actions and continued, or prompted others to try some of the same. It is important that counselors on campuses where racial incidents happen become a part of the vocal majority and put a stop to such behavior. One should not whisper about the situation but be prepared to speak firmly and forthrightly at once. Being an advocate for your students sometimes requires a bold commitment to a set of beliefs that foster goodwill. Remember, your black clients will be watching your personal behavior throughout any such ordeals.

Racial incidents on campus underscore the need for the institution to establish preventive and corrective measures for negative behavior. If a program or policy that addresses racial and ethnic harassment is not present on campus, counselors can become the catalyst for starting the discussion at the highest possible administrative level. Policies of this type should, as the regents of the University of Oklahoma recently announced, "prohibit conduct or speech that is directed at the race, religion, ethnicity, or national origin of individuals that is intended to 'inflict harm'." It further banned slander, libel, or obscene speech based on race. Appropriate punishments ranged from simple reprimands to expulsion for students who violate the policy. Each campus needs a policy which is explicit and practiced by all. In the event where the policy fails to motivate the guilty, the administration should have a procedure ready to involve the local police authority for either civil or criminal prosecution.

I would simply caution that any campus policy is only one part of the solution to racial problems. There is a need, in addition, for students, faculty, staff, and alumni to help black students feel comfortable on campus by just being friendly. All it takes is a smile or a "hello" when passing on campus or the sharing of a table at meals. Many opportunities exist in the dormitories for students to develop good personal relationships -- some of which may last for a lifetime. When racial tension increases on a campus, that is an excellent time to urge the use of more courses that address the diversity in race and culture found in the student body. There are national academe arguments going on which speak to the need for "American cultures" courses, even beginning with Freshman-level composition. Some emphasis is being placed on teaching the history, significance, and consequences of the beautiful cultures found in America.

Counselors should be aware of the naming of committees on campus that have the responsibility to plan cultural or history courses based in the racial, ethnic, or religious makeup of America. If it is not possible for the counselor to become a member of the committee, then at least appear before it with some ideas or proposals to help shape the direction. You will be amazed at the amount of naiveté to be found on such committees when the topics of race or ethnicity are discussed. As a campus change agent who is in daily, personal, one-to-one contact with students, your voice should be heard.

SPORTS AS AN AVENUE TO HIGHER EDUCATION

This topic is perhaps one of the more explosive to face college presidents in many years. When sports are viewed as an educational tool for those with athletic ability, it is possible to facilitate a student's entrance into college. Some proponents feel that academics and sports go hand in hand. Those on the other side prefer to keep them separate in the belief that the concept of a "student athlete" is at least an oxymoron among the many we find in academe. Much has been written on the poor academic performance of many popular college athletes. A few sensational cases of student athletes who left college with a degree and were not able to read have been brought before a shocked public. It appears that some coaches and athletic directors recruited poor students who were outstanding on the playing fields, just for their athletic prowess. They have been accused of exploiting the young people in order to have a powerhouse team and to win. Some sports figures have blatantly said that if the student could not keep up with the academics, then it is not the fault of the athletic program. In defense of the college program, other coaches have pointed with pride to the number of their athletes who do graduate and succeed in life.

Over the decade of the Eighties, the National Collegiate Athletic Association has had its agenda full with pleas for reforms. Several controversial propositions were heard and some adopted by the board. One, in particular, speaks to the level of SAT scores and college entrance requirements. Many colleges protested that this rule would eliminate black athletes since they do not test well. By the end of 1990, there were at least thirty institutions under NCAA sanctions for infractions of the rules. The violations included: giving cash to players; lack of institutional control; playing academically ineligible students; and academic fraud.

These deviations from the norm do serious damage to the idea of sports accessing higher education. Many young people are good athletes and good students too, so they should be allowed to approach college in this manner. The argument for poor students to be forgiven the academic requirements is not accepted by faculty and administrators. College presidents who do not have charge of their athletic departments suffer greatly when a rule is broken or an athlete dropped for academic reasons. They also find it difficult to explain the violent coach's behavior at sports events. Perhaps it is because the program brings in so much money from the games, television rights, and endorsements. Sports can be of help, but it requires regulation and careful use.

THIRTEEN

BLACK STUDENT CASE STUDIES

The following composite cases of black college students are presented to demonstrate the variety and complexity of problems experienced as they attended predominantly white institutions of higher learning. They were selected from the author's own professional practice and from the student bodies of both urban and residential campuses. It is not my intention to suggest that they should be considered typical, or representative of blacks everywhere. Rather, they should be considered as study practice cases, from which you may gain insights into the inter-relatedness of the social, educational, economic, and emotional facets of black people. It is my hope that these few illustrations will lead you to ask: **"How would I counsel effectively with a student like this? What may I offer him or her in terms of myself and that which the institution has provided? When can I expect to see the results of my work with the student? Why does one student respond positively and another negatively? How do I prepare myself to better serve the black clients I work with each day?"**

I invite you to take the time not only to read these cases but to analyze them for the vast array of problems, changes, adaptations, and other actions black students are subject to on a longitudinal personal development time line. Perhaps with close examination you will gather some of the aforementioned insights to enhance your own understanding and set new or improved directions for your counseling behavior in the future. If these cases prompt you to make change for the better, then both you and your students should reap some lasting benefits.

CASE STUDIES

Michael J.

Michael had to be called into the counseling office with a letter from the Dean which stated that his current enrollment was in jeopardy because of last semester's low grades. The student appeared angry and stated that he did not know of his low grades because the mail was not delivered to his house. It was now about one-third through the following semester. He could not explain why he was not at least curious about his final grades to ask before now. He "assumed" that they were all right.

The counselor explained the seriousness of the academic deficiency which put Michael on the edge of being dismissed. Michael repeated his original statement that the University was responsible for his problem by not sending out his grades.

A "contract" was agreed upon by the counselor and Michael which indicated that he was currently enrolled in six semester hours and would have to make a 2.50 semester G.P.A. in order to continue in college. After signing the contract, Michael left the office without making any plans for future semesters. He was clearly angry.

DISCUSSION:
WAS A CONTRACT NECESSARY? WHY, WHY NOT?
WHAT DO YOU DO NEXT?
HOW DO YOU REDUCE THE STUDENT'S ANGER?

128

Shalanda G.

Shalanda is a nineteen-year-old female who lives in a
low-rent housing project with her mother, two younger
sisters, and an older brother who dropped out of school
at age sixteen and cannot find work. She told the
counselor that she was late for the appointment because
there was a big family argument over her brother's
inability to work and contribute to the household. It
appeared that she was the only family member to stand-
up for him. She, of course, neglected to check the time
of day and missed the public bus which would have gotten
her to campus on time.

When the counselor felt that Shalanda had finished the
explanation for being late, he proceeded to ask her about
academic matters, leading up to the low mid-term grades
just issued to all entering freshmen. Her name was on
the list. Shalanda expressed surprise at the notice and
said that she did not receive the notice at home through
the mail. She appeared distressed at the news and
immediately said, "I'll try harder." The counselor
suggested that perhaps she needed to review her study
habits as one measure of correcting the problem.
Shalanda then admitted that it was very difficult to
study at home because of the lack of privacy. She shares
a bedroom with her two sisters who like to play noisy
games and listen to loud music all the time. When the
counselor suggested further that Shalanda try studying at
the campus library, she found that impossible, too, since
she does not have a car and the buses stop running in her
neighborhood after five o'clock.

DISCUSSION:
HOW DO YOU ADVISE HER?
WHAT CAN BE DONE FOR THE HOME SITUATION?
SHOULD SHALANDA BE REFERRED? TO WHAT OFFICE?

Thomas R.

This student came into the office for an appointment on time. He seemed a little out of breath but settled down quickly and began to busily look through his notebook for a paper which turned out to be a list of courses for a degree in business. He was anxious to enter the School of Business but had not completed all of the requirements. His record folder showed a G.P.A. of 2.75 which was adequate for entrance to his chosen school. Thomas's high school record indicated a total of 950 on the SAT but only one year of algebra, and that was in the ninth grade. While writing his name on a check sheet for the school of business, the student corrected the counselor -- "Thomas" -- not "Tom!" There was no belligerence in his voice, but he got the point across.

This student did not seem to have any outstanding problems and was currently enrolled full time while working 20 to 30 hours a week as a waiter in a downtown cafe. He needs the money to supplement both his Pell Grant and what his widowed mother can provide toward his education.

Thomas was planning to enroll in a finite math course next semester and asked me to describe the course for him. The counselor gave him the bulletin which had the course descriptions and suggested that he read it for himself. Thomas said he was not ready for that course because he "hated" mathematics and wondered if he could put it off until his junior year.

DISCUSSION:
WHAT ARE THE NEXT STEPS FOR THOMAS? DETAIL THEM.
HOW WOULD TIME MANAGEMENT HELP THIS STUDENT?
WHAT CAN YOU SAY TO ENCOURAGE THOMAS IN HIS QUEST FOR
ACADEMIC SUCCESS?

Alice R.

Alice is the type of student all the colleges want to recruit. She had excellent test scores, high rank, plenty of motivation, and college-trained parents who are both professionals. It was expected that Alice would go to college and that it would be her own choice. She was admitted on the basis of six semesters of high school course work and the recommendation of her principal. Her major choice is nursing.

Coming from a family of three children, Alice is the oldest and, of course, is the first one to enter college. She immediately began preparation after graduation from high school with a "How-to-Study-in-College" course taught that summer on the local campus of the State University. That fall Alice went to the main campus and started living in a coed dorm.

Alice did well in her laboratory and humanities courses. She seemed to have few problems to deal with on campus and maintained a G.P.A. of 3.25. Second semester, she joined her mother's sorority which has high prestige within the national black community. Her mother and father visited her at campus only during special times when Alice was a part of a public program. Both parents felt it was the right way to relate to "a grown daughter" -- give her the space and responsibility of living away from home. Alice's sisters visited her on "Homecoming Day" and enjoyed staying in a college dorm room.

When it was time for Alice to enter the clinical phase of her nursing training, she had to move to University's Metropolitan Campus in the state's largest city. This was a new experience for her since her own hometown was smaller and less congested.

Alice had experienced some racial discrimination at the main campus by fellow students and by the drama coach who said Alice's very dark skin "was not right for the part of Antigone in a Greek tragedy." She also felt that her white patients in the hospital treated her "like a maid." She went to the School's Counseling

Office to complain. The counselor she talked to advised her "to keep a low profile."

Alice met and started dating a young, black intern at the hospital who was from out of state. By the time she was in the second half of her senior year, Alice was engaged to the young man and was planning a Christmas wedding. Unfortunately, Alice was not passed in all of her clinicals. She said that "it was impossible to concentrate" on her work because of the racist atmosphere "on the floor" at the hospital. She returned to the Counseling Office for help.

DISCUSSION:
HOW CAN THIS STUDENT BE SAVED?
WHAT WOULD YOU DO ABOUT THE CHARGES OF RACISM?
SHOULD ALICE'S PARENTS CONFRONT YOU ABOUT THE
EXPRESSED DIFFICULTIES, WHAT DO YOU SAY?

Beverly B.

Beverly is now twenty-six years old. She began college at age nineteen -- just out of high school. The college Admissions Office granted her admission into the developmental program which gives students with low entrance credits but high potential a single semester of special courses designed to improve certain academic skills. Beverly was successful in that first semester and proceeded to the second with careful counseling. For some unknown reason, Beverly withdrew about one-third of the way into the second semester. There was no exit interview or warning of the sudden departure.

On registration day, Beverly returned for what should have become her third semester at college and enrolled in twelve semester hours. Because she was working part-time, Beverly dropped six of the credits in the hope of adjusting better to the academic environment. When talking to her counselor, Beverly said that it was

132

necessary for her to work and help her mother with the household expenses. It seemed that the mother and father had divorced just a few months before, and Beverly has not seen her father since he left the house. Beverly continued to enroll and drop courses for the next six semesters and all summer sessions until she had accumulated more than 120 credits. All this time she maintained a 2.00 G.P.A. or better. Unfortunately, the courses do not form a degree program, which leaves Beverly still searching. She told her counselor that teacher education was her goal and would continue to pursue it until finished. She now has a job as a teacher's aide in a public school in town, and she just loves working with the kids.

During one of her absences from college, Beverly gave birth to a baby whose father was her steady boyfriend. No paternity has been established. Her mother continues to work but is sick a lot. Beverly seems unable to complete a full semester of course work and shows evidence of emotional problems.

DISCUSSION:
HOW DO YOU CONTINUE AS HER COUNSELOR?
DO YOU EXPECT THIS STUDENT TO PERSIST? WHY, WHY NOT?
WHAT OTHER KIND OF HELP DOES BEVERLY NEED?

SUMMARY
and Counselor Guide

The important theses and facts presented in this book can be summarized as follows: empathetic understanding plus a good knowledge of client social sciences will provide a springboard for effective relationship development. This is critical, even when the differing conditions of race or culture enter the counseling session.

College officials, faculty, staff, and counselors who are white need to commit to the idea of blending the social sciences and culture of black students into their own consciousness. Such action will foster a better understanding and appreciation of the beautiful differences found in all humans. Now is the time for colleges to recognize the need for, and work at the enhancement of, black student enrollment. In doing so, higher educational opportunities can be made more easily available. Recruitment and financial aid should become co-priorities for the last of the Eighties and on into the Nineties. Funding sources will find it difficult to finance all the needs which face both private and public institutions of higher learning. Somehow, the mission must be accomplished if this country is to continue to enjoy a favored leadership role among the nations of the world.

The following **"Counselor Behavior Reminders"** will serve the caring counselor as a helpful referral list for that important advising journey with your students of color:

134

COUNSELOR
BEHAVIOR REMINDERS

1. Realize that a difference in race and color is present in your client and yourself, then accept it.

2. Use your counseling skills and capitalize on the differences for positive results.

3. Read to learn about the social sciences of your black clients.

4. Reject the pathological approach in the helping process. Have positive expectations that are realistic.

5. Give your best and expect the best in order to get the best from your student.

6. Practice empathy and use special knowledge instead of relying on sympathy and myths.

7. Accept that you will not be a 100% winner each time in helping your students -- but never stop trying!

8. Consider each black client as the most important person in your professional life at the time you are relating to each other.

9. You should "see" the color of your client's skin and use that information to work effectively with him or her as a caring academic counselor.

10. Remember that many black students will come to your (predominantly white) campus not having experienced such a milieu before. There may be fear, shyness, loneliness, or even anger as they try to adjust to a new environment. You should be one of the "campus helpers."

11. As rumors, myths, and stereotypes circulate through the campus, try to stop them by not participating in their spread.

12. Build a comprehensive referral list which you keep current and available. While you may not personally aid a student with a problem, there may be others who can.

13. Racist thoughts and acts are damaging to the victim and are reflective of past socialization. You need to change your attitude.

14. Develop a collection of pertinent career materials for use by your black clients.

15. Teach coping skills to your students who may be having difficulty relating to professors and their differing classroom styles.

136

BIBLIOGRAPHY

Allport, Gordon W. The Nature of Prejudice. Garden City, NY: Doubleday, 1958.

American Council on Education. Minorities on Campus: A Handbook for Enhancing Diversity. Washington, D.C.: 1989.

Anastasi, Anne. Psychological Testing. New York: Macmillan, 1976.

Astin, Alexander W. Minorities in American Higher Education. San Francisco: Jossey-Bass, 1982.

Berry, Mary F. and Blassingame, John W. Long Memory. The Black American Experience. New York: Oxford Univ. Press, 1982.

The Bible. Revised Standard Version.

Billingsley, Andrew. Black Families in White America. Englewood Cliffs, NJ: Prentice-Hall, 1968.

Blackwell, James E. The Black Community. New York: Dodd, Mead & Co., 1975.

_____, and Hart, Philip. Cities, Suburbs and Blacks. Bayside, NY: General Hall, Inc., 1982.

Benedict, Ruth. Race, Science and Politics. rev. ed. New York: Viking, 1978.

Bogardus, Emory S. Social Distance. Yellow Springs, OH: Antioch Press, 1959.

Boyd, William M. II. "Today's Black Students: A Success Story." AGB Reports, Sept/Oct 1979.

Brown, Robert S. and Rustin, Bayard. "Separation or Integration: Which Way for America" in Three Perspectives on Ethnicity edited by Carlos Cortez et al. New York: G. P. Putnam's Sons, 1976.

Brown vs. Topeka Board of Education, U.S. Supreme Court Decision, 1954.

Bynum, Alvin S. "Counseling is Key to Negro Achievement," Hoosier Schoolmaster, Terre Haute, IN, 1964.

Bynum, Marie S. "Black Identity." (Unpublished paper) 1970.

Carnegie Council on Policy Studies in Higher Education: Making Affirmative Action Work in Higher Education. San Francisco: Jossey-Bass, 1975.

Chickering, Arthur W. Education and Identity. San Francisco: Jossey-Bass, 1969.

Clark, Kenneth B. Dark Ghetto. New York: Harper & Row, 1965.

_____ and Clark, Mamie. "What Do Blacks Think of Themselves?", Ebony, Nov., 1980.

Collison, Michele. "More young black men choosing not to go to college." Chronicle of Higher Education, Dec. 9, 1987.

Comer, James P. M.D. Beyond Black and White. New York: Quadrangle Books, 1972.

Cooley, Charles H. Human Nature and the Social Order. New York: Scribner, 1922.

Cox, Oliver. Caste, Class and Race. New York: Modern Reader Paperbacks, 1970 & 1948.

Cruse, Harold. The Crisis of the Negro Intellectual. New York: William Morrow, 1967.

Dollard, John. Caste and Class in a Southern Town. New Haven: Yale Univ. Press, 1937.

Drake, St. Clair and Cayton, Horace. Black Metropolis. New York: Harper & Row, 1962.

DuBois, W.E.B. A W.E.B. Dubois Reader. edited by Andrew G. Paschal. New York: Collier Books, 1971.

_____ The Souls of Black Folk. New York: New American Library, 1969.

Edwards, G. Franklin. The Negro Professional Class. Glencoe, IL: The Free Press, 1959.

Ellison, Ralph. The Invisible Man. New York: Random House, 1952.

Erikson, Erik H. Identity, Youth and Crisis. New York: W. W. Norton, 1968.

Feldman, Saul D. and Thielbar, Gerald W. Life Styles: Diversity in American Society. Boston: Little Brown & Co., 1972.

Fleming, Jacqueline. Blacks in College. San Francisco: Jossey-Bass, 1984.

Franklin, John Hope. From Slavery to Freedom. (6th ed.) New York: McGraw-Hill, 1987.

Frazier, E. Franklin. Black Bourgeoisie. London: Collier Books, 1969.

Garibaldi, Antoine. Black Colleges and Universities, Challenges for the Future. New York: Praeger, 1984.

Gibbs, J. "Black Students/White University: Different Expectations." Personnel and Guidance Journal, 1973, 51, 463-469.

Ginzberg, Eli. The Middle Class Negro in the White Man's World. New York: Columbia Univ. Press, 1967.

Glasser, William. Reality Therapy. New York: Harper & Row, 1965.

Glazer, Nathan and Moynihan, Daniel P. Beyond the Melting Pot. Cambridge, MA: The MIT Press, 1963.

Gordon, Joan. The Poor of Harlem: Social Functioning in the Underclass, (New York: Report, Office of the Mayor, 1965).

Gregg, Sandra. "Paucity of black men stymies collegiate environment. "Black Issues In Higher Education. (Feb. 2, 1989).

Grier, William H. and Cobbs, Price M. Black Rage. New York: Bantam Books, 1968.

Gutman, Herbert G. The Black Family in Slavery and Freedom, 1750-1925. New York: Pantheon Books, 1976.

Gwaltney, John L. Drylongso. New York: Random House, 1980.

Hale, Janice. "Childrearing in Black Families." (Paper given at ACABC in Higher Ed.) 1980.

Haley, Alex. Roots: The Saga of an American Family. Garden City, NY: Doubleday, 1974.

Harper, Frederick. Black Students: White Campus. Washington, D.C. APGA, 1975.

Hill, Robert. The Strengths of Black Families. New York: Emerson Hall, Pub., 1972.

Hughes, Langston. Selected Poems. New York: Knopf, 1975.

Jaynes, Gerald D. and Williams, Robin M. Jr., Eds. A Common Destiny: Blacks and American Society. Washington, D.C.: National Academy Press, 1989.

Jencks, Christopher. Inequality. New York: Basic Books, 1972.

Johnson, Roosevelt. Black Agenda for Career Education. Columbus, OH: ECCA Pub. 1974.

Jones, Major J. Black Awareness: A Theology of Hope. Nashville: Abingdon Press, 1971.

Jones, Reginald, ed. Black Psychology. New York: Harper & Row, 1972.

Journal of Negro Education, Vol. XLIX, No. 3, Howard University, Washington, D.C., Summer 1980. (Critical issues in testing)

Kardiner, A. and Ovesey, L. The Mark of Oppression. Cleveland: World Pub. Co. 1951, 1967.

Karinga, Maulana. Introduction to Black Studies. Los Angeles: Sancore Press, 1989.

Keller, George. "Black students in higher education: Why so few?" Planning for Higher Education, vol. 17, no. 3, 1988-89.

Killens, John Oliver. "Explanation of the Black Psyche." in Three Perspectives on Ethnicity. ed. by Cortis, C. E., Ginsburg, A. D., Green, A. W. F., Joseph, J. A. New York: Putnam's Sons, 1976.

King, Coretta Scott. The Words of Martin Luther King, Jr. New York: New Market Press, 1983.

King, Martin Luther, Jr. Where Do We Go From Here? New York: Bantam Books, 1968.

Liebow, Elliot. Tally's Corner. Boston: Little, Brown & Co. 1967.

Lincoln, C. Eric. The Negro Pilgrimage in America. New York: Bantam Books, 1973.

McAdoo, Harriette Pipes. "Black Kinship," in Psychology Today. May, 1979.

_____, ed. Black Families. Beverly Hills, CA: Sage Pub. 1981.

Martin, Elmer P. and Martin, Joanne M. The Black Extended Family. Chicago: Univ. of Chicago Press, 1978.

Meltzer, Milton. The Black Americans. New York: Harper & Row, 1984.

Merton, Robert K. Sociological Ambivalence. New York: Macmillan Pub., 1976.

Milliken, R. "Prejudice and Counseling Effectiveness." Personnel and Guidance Journal, 43 (1965), 710-712.

Myrdal, Gunnar. An American Dilemma: The Negro Problem and Modern Democracy. New York: Harper and Row, 1944.

National Urban League. "The State of Black American Families". (a report, New York, 1985, 1986).

_____. The State of Black America, 1990. New York: 1990.

Owens, William A. Slave Mutiny. New York: Day Co., 1953.

Pauk, Walter. How to Study In College. 2nd ed. Boston: Houghton-Mifflin, 1974.

Poussaint, Alvin F. Are the New Lifestyles Shortchanging the Children? Milwaukee: Univ. of Wisconsin, 1977.

Quarles, Benjamin. The Negro in the Making of America. New York: Collier Books, 1964.

Raspberry, William. "Blacks and Higher Education." Indianapolis Star, 21 July 1987, p. 17.

Rogers, Carl. Client-Centered Therapy. Boston: Houghton Mifflin, 1951.

_____. On Becoming a Person. New York: Houghton Mifflin, 1951.

_____. "The Characteristics of a Helping Relationship." Personnel and Guidance Journal, 37, (1958), 6-16.

_____. "The Interpersonal Relationship": The Core of Guidance. Harvard Educational Review, No. 32, (1962).

Rossides, Daniel W. The American Class System. Boston: Houghton Mifflin, 1970.

Rustin, Bayard. Down The Line. Chicago: Quadrangle Books, 1971.

Sillen, S., Thomas, A. Racism and Psychiatry. New York: Mazel, Inc. 1972.

Smith, Paul M. "Counseling from the Past and Present with Blacks!" The Journal of Negro Education. 43, (Feb. 1974), 489-493.

Staples, Robert. Introduction to Black Sociology. San Francisco: McGraw-Hill, 1976.

_____. Black Masculinity: The Black Male's Role in American Society. San Francisco: The Black Scholar Press, 1982.

Stikes, C. Scully. Black Students in Higher Education. Carbondale, IL: Southern Illinois Univ. Press, 1984.

Terry, Wallace. Bloods. New York: Random House, 1984.

Urban League. The State of Black America 1990. Dewart, Janet, Editor. New York: 1990.

U.S. Census Report. Washington, D.C. U.S. Government Printing Office, 1960, 1970, 1980.

U.S. National Advisory Commission on Civil Disorders. ("Kerner Report") New York: Dutton, 1968.

Vontress, Clemmont E. "Counseling Blacks." Personnel and Guidance Journal. May 1970, Vol. 48, No. 9.

_____. "Counseling Negroes." in Guidance Monograph Series. (Vol. 6) Shertzer, B. and Stone, S. (eds.) Boston: Houghton Mifflin, 1971.

Washington, Kenneth R. "White Counselors and Black Students: An analysis of the Problems Faced By Each." Notre Dame Journal of Education. (Winter, 1973: 4), 322-327.

Williams, Juan. Eyes on the Prize. NY: Penguin Books, 1988.

Willie, Charles Vert. A New Look at Black Families. 3rd Ed. Dix Hills, NY: General Hall, Inc. 1988.

Wilson, William Julius. The Declining Significance of Race. Chicago: Univ. of Chicago Press, 1978.

Winston, Roger B. et al. Developmental Academic Advising. San Francisco: Jossey-Bass, 1984.

Wright, Richard. American Hunger. New York: Harper and Row, 1977.

_____ Native Son. New York: Harper and Row, 1940.

AN ANNOTATED READING LIST
OF BLACK AMERICAN LIFE

Adams, Russell L., <u>Great Negroes Past and Present</u>,
Chicago, Afro-American Pub. Co., 1964.

A collection of vignettes relating accomplishments
of many prominent Black Americans with
pencil/charcoal portraits.

Bennett, Lerone, Jr., <u>Before the Mayflower</u>, Baltimore,
Penguin Books, 1966.

An excellent historical view of black presence in
America before the Pilgrims through slavery and into
freedom. Well documented and illustrated with
pictures from the National Archives and other
collections.

Berry, Mary Frances and Blassingame, John W., <u>Long
Memory</u>, New York, N.Y. Oxford University Press, 1982.

A history of the black experience in America with
photos and cartoons from early publications.

Billingsley, Andrew, <u>Black Families in White America</u>,
Englewood Cliffs, New Jersey, Prentice-Hall, 1968.

A black social scientist provides answers to many of
the questions surrounding the Black American family's
development.

Blackwell, James E., <u>The Black Community</u>, New York,
Dodd and Mead & Co. 1975.

A view of the Black Community as a diverse group of
people in terms of social class, life styles, and
attitudes.

Chapman, Abraham, ed., Black Voices, New York, Mentor Books, 1968.

An anthology of "traditional" poetry by Black Americans describing the frustrations and hopes of a segregated people.

-------, New Black Voices, New York, Mentor Books, 1972.

An anthology of contemporary poetry by young Black Americans covering the "Sixties."

Franklin, John Hope, From Slavery to Freedom, (6th ed. New York, McGraw-Hill, Inc., 1987.

A widely used history of Black Americans written by a distinguished black historian. A classic in the field.

Frazier, E. Franklin, Black Bourgeoisie, London, Collier Books, 1962, (first pub. 1957, by the Free Press).

A controversial study by a leading black sociologist which describes the rise of the black middle class in the U.S.

Grier, William H., and Cobbs, Price M., Black Rage, New York, Bantam Books, Inc. 1968.

Authored by two black psychiatrists, it reveals the full dimensions of the emotional conflicts and desperation of the black man in America. It examines the struggle to achieve manhood and womanhood.

Gutman, Herbert G. The Black Family in Slavery and Freedom, 1750-1925. New York, Pantheon Books, 1976.

The author found and studied slave records, diaries, and other documents to trace family groups from bondage to freepersons.

Jaynes, Gerald D. and Williams, Robin M. Jr., Eds. A
     Common Destiny: Blacks and American Society.
     Washington, D.C.: National Academy Press, 1989.

     An intensive, four-year study of the successes and
     hardships of American blacks since 1939. "Is the
     glass of racial progress half empty or half full?"

Hill, Robert B., The Strengths of Black Families, New
     York, Emerson Hall Pub., 1971.

     A National Urban League research study which
     attempts to strip away the myths and stereotypes in
     America which result in "blaming the victim."

Pinkney, Alphonso, Black Americans, Englewood Cliffs,
     N.J. Prentice-Hall, Inc., 1975, 2nd Ed.

     One in a series of descriptive and analytical
     overviews of American heritage.

Quarles, Benjamin, The Negro in the Making of America,
     New York, Macmillan Co., 1968.

     An impressive account of Black American
     contributions to the nation's development from
     slavery through modern times.

Staples, Robert, Introduction to Black Sociology, San
     Francisco, McGraw-Hill, 1976.

     A basic book for the study of the social sciences of
     Black Americans in the context of the wider society.

COMMUNITY RESOURCE LIST

Agency Name	Address	Telephone	Contact

In the helping relationship, counselors need to remain prepared to give clients appropriate referrals when the current office visit is not enough. Care should be taken not to allow the pressure of time or lack of enthusiasm to dictate whether you help the client at that immediate time or send them to another source. Resist the ever-present urge to "pass the buck" because you are tired or busy.

To help deal with the need for preparedness, a "Community Resource List" is formatted above. Use it as a guide if your local community does not have a printed list or book available. Check with the United Way Community Services Council office. They should be able to direct you to many helpful materials and services which your students can use. You might also find it more convenient to use 3 X 5 cards which should make it easy to alphabetize the list.

Once you have developed a list of your own, be sure to keep it current. Nothing is more frustrating for a student than to accept the referral and then discover upon travelling across town that the source of help has moved or that the person to see is no longer there. Telephone numbers also change perhaps more often than most of us would like it to happen.

In addition to having a valid list, it is important to know the resource. Having knowledge of each of the sources will certainly enhance your decision on which one to use in which circumstance. Get to know the people at the source so that your student will benefit from the new relationship.

A HOLISTIC PROCESS FOR ACADEMIC COUNSELING

Portals for Students
to Enter the Advising Process in College:

LIFE GOALS EXPLORATION

CAREER GOALS EXPLORATION   TRANSCRIPT REVIEW

Counseling
Session

CHOICE OF COURSES   SCHEDULING COURSES

CHOICE OF MAJOR

The student seeking academic counseling may choose to enter the relationship with a counselor through any one of the portals of the holistic process. It is the express responsibility of the counselor to identify and accept the student's current life position then to proceed together on an informative, caring journey to help him or her achieve a desired academic goal. After receiving desired assistance, the student should find it comfortable to exit the process through an appropriate portal when personal satisfaction is reached or when the counselor makes a mutually agreed upon referral to another source of help.

Life Goals Exploration:
  -Know your student's background and social sciences of his or her ethnic/cultural group.
  -Use your various skills in counseling techniques.
  -Recognize and appreciate the differences in people.
  -If necessary, teach student the decision-making process.
  -Believe that all people have potential, dignity, and individual worth. Your client should be able to perceive this in all that you say or do.

Career Goals Exploration:
  -Know career fields and their potential for the present and the immediate future.
  -Use skills as needed for preparation for student's taking personal assessment tests.
  -Examine why student does or does not prefer a specific career direction.
  -Use all other counselor skills.

Choice of Courses:
  -Know institutional rules and regulations.
  -Know courses, instructors and teaching styles.
  -Review records to determine student's potential academic ability.
  -Be familiar with course content as stated in the college bulletin. In addition, share any special information from the course department with the student.
  -Refer student to honors or developmental courses, or to tutors, as appropriate.

Choice of Major:
  -Know the majors and minors available at the college.
  -Know the prerequisites.

-Know the requirements to enter the school or major of choice. Give this to student in written form (i.e., checksheet or program bulletin).
-Know the career area of the chosen major. Be familiar with the type of work, salary, working conditions, persons successful in that field, etc.
-Permit student to make a wise major choice based on correct information which you supply.

Scheduling Classes:
-Have schedule of classes available. Know how to find courses in it quickly. Plan appropriate courses on paper with student.
-Teach student how to use the schedule efficiently.
-Remind student to consider the importance of work time, travel time, and personal life time in the building of a good schedule.
-Put student to work on the schedule, preferably outside your office, so that you can see other students and do other work. Encourage the student to return for confirmation and counselor's O.K., if necessary.

Transcript Review:
-Examine high school and college grades, courses, test scores, etc., for student academic   potential.
-Share contents of folder with student to confirm academic status.
-Encourage student to keep a current copy of own transcript and other college records in a safe place at home.

(Source: The O'Banion Model, "A Process Paradigm")

PERSONAL ACTION PLAN

At the conclusion of reading this book, (or completing
the author's "Seminar in Black and White"), each person
should begin to formulate his/her own "Personal Action
Plan" based on what you have learned. Photocopy this
page -- Complete your Plan -- Put it away in an envelope
to be opened and read one semester later to see what
changes you recognize in your counselor behavior.
----
1. I can now begin to see black students as. . .

2. I no longer think that all blacks are. . .

3. As I work with black students I will attempt to. . .

4. When I have racist thoughts in the future. . .

5. Before black students ask me for career information,
   I shall. . .

6. When racist stories circulate around the campus, my
   role is to. . .

7. I now believe that racial, cultural, or color
   differences can. . .

8. I shall respond to the hostile black student in my
   office by. . .

9. With black students as my counselees I can now. . .

10. Realizing that everything I need to know cannot be
learned in one seminar or by the reading of one book, I
shall continue my education in the social sciences of
the Black Community by. . .

INDEX